THE
RAILWAY ERA

THE RAILWAY ERA

life and lines in the Great Age of Railways

Geoffrey Body

British Library Cataloguing
in Publication Data

Body, Geoffrey
    The Railway Era
    1. Great Britain - Social life and customs -
        19th century
    2. Great Britain - Social life and customs -
        20th century
    I. Title
    941.081   DA533

ISBN 0 86190 072 3

Printed in the U.K. by
Butler and Tanner Ltd, Frome
for Moorland Publishing Company Ltd,
PO Box 2, 9-11 Station Street, Ashbourne,
Derbyshire, DE6 1DZ, England

CONTENTS

ILLUSTRATIONS

Notes and Acknowledgements

In presenting this picture of the immense variety and vitality of railways in their heyday some slight liberties have been taken with strict chronology in order to give a true composite impression. For the same reason, and to add to the atmosphere, the language of the period has been retained in the fairly extensive quotations from contemporary reports and regulations, and money is expressed in its original pounds, shillings and pence, leaving the reader to make the conversion on the basis of 12d to 5p.

By referring to railway activities in the the past tense I would not want to detract from the achievements of British Rail today. This may well be 'The Age of the Train' but in this, as in many other spheres, the pursuit of speed and efficiency has lost us something of past colour and atmosphere — as well as past discomforts!

I warmly acknowledge the considerable help with information and research provided by Charles Clinker and Richard Body and would also like to record my appreciation of the assistance afforded to me by John Scott, the British Rail regions and many others who have helped with data and illustrations.

Sources of illustrations:
Avon County Library/Woodspring Central Library: p 117; BBC Hulton Picture Library: p 86-7, 105; E.N. Bellass: p 79, 80 (upper), 96 (upper), 106, 131, 136; British Rail (ER): p 41, 50, 51, 58, 59, 69 (upper), 129; British Rail (LMR): p 43, 66, 70; British Rail (WR): p 48-9, 90-1, 120, 149; H.C. Casserley Collection: p 64, 71, 116, 123, 145, 146; J.A. Fleming: p 68, 93; M.E. Graeme: p 89; *Illustrated London News:* p 12, 14, 17, 18, 20, 22, 27, 30, 31, 34, 37, 135 (upper), 141 (upper left); Lens of Sutton: p 42, 44, 102 (lower), 109, 113, 119, 126; Liverpool Central Library: p 26, 28-9; Manchester Model Railway Society: p 24, 39, 52; T. Nicholls: p 110; G.H. Soole: p 57 (lower), 60-1, 62, 63, 67, 69 (lower), 74-5, 76 (upper), 85, 98, 105 (lower), 135 (lower), 150-1; J.W. Walker: p 76 (lower); G. Walwyn: p 81; the remaining illustrations are from the author's collection.

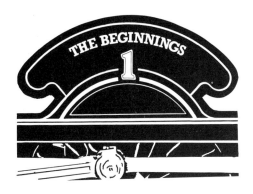

By 1920 Great Britain had over 20,000 miles of main line railway and trains were a part of everyone's life. But a century earlier few had seen or heard of railways, fewer still understood that the use of railed vehicles could reduce friction and increase payloads, and only a tiny number cared one way or another. The age was one in which the lower classes struggled to find work, received little for their long hours and found relief only on the Sabbath or in the pot house and gin parlour. The agricultural worker, used to seeing the fruits of his labours moved by pack horse or carrier's wagon, would not have believed that a new transport system was about to change a nation in his lifetime. His fellow worker in the factory, with any energy he had to spare for thought after a 12-14 hour day, would have seen the canal system as quite adequate for the movement of the products on which he laboured.

Railways of a sort existed at least as early as 1603 and many short tramways were subsequently built to link mines and quarries with a nearby waterway, but over 200 years were to elapse before they made any sort of impact upon the community at large. Then, in the short space of 25 years, a new transport network was to emerge and not only link London with the South Coast, Bristol, the Midlands, North West and North East but also have towns clamouring to be added to the 5,000 miles of railway already built for fear that the advantages brought by the shining metals would pass them by.

Great Britain started its period of dramatic change soon after the middle of the eighteenth century. Between 1764 and 1785 the progressive introduction of the spinning jenny, waterframe and mule to Lancashire's cotton industry had increased output and stimulated a demand for raw cotton, and similar changes were taking place in other trades and industries. In 1784 John Palmer introduced his fast, light mail coaches to help to meet the demand for faster communication and many canals put on 'fly boats' which had priority over all other canal traffic and eventually produced speeds averaging 10mph or more. Some 4,000 turnpike or similar Acts helped to improve the nation's road system and the first road engineers, 'Blind Jack' Metcalfe and then Thomas Telford, began the process of changing roads from compacted soil and stones to graded level surfaces, well drained and lying on a good foundation. John Loudon McAdam was to do even more for the road network from 1816 onwards but the nation's industrial revolution was taking place faster than its transport could cope with.

Important as the opening of the Stockton and Darlington Railway was in 1825 and however much the Liverpool and Manchester enterprise might have heralded the dawn of the inter-city network in 1830, Great Britain's railway system did not spring up overnight, nor was its advent met with either universal interest or acclaim. True, there were plenty of omens — the opening of the Surrey Iron Railway in 1803, passenger carrying by the Oystermouth Railway from 1807 and the steam locomotive work of men like Trevithick, Blenkinsop and Murray — but the wars of the first years of the century tended to overshadow such minor and localised happenings. In any event, newspapers were few, circulations limited and prices high. Moreover, the vast majority of the population could not read. *The Times* and *The Observer* had been circulating among the wealthy and learned since the end of the eighteenth century but the *Guardian* was not born, as the *Manchester Guardian,* until 1821 and some years were still to pass before the first edition of the *News of the World* or the launch of *The Daily News* with Charles Dickens as its editor and undercutting *The Times* by 2d a copy.

Even after the end of the Napoleonic Wars times remained difficult. The National Debt had rocketed to £800m as a result of the long period of hostilities, and the extravagances of the Prince of Wales added further to the financial burden falling upon the country. With a succession of bad harvests, a Poor Law which related a labourer's relief to the size of his family and a continuing displacement of men by machinery the stage was set for a decade of unrest. This duly followed in 1811 when, in a fit of passion, one Ned Ludd broke two stocking frames and sparked off a wave of Luddite destruction in Lancashire, Yorkshire and the Midlands. A succession of other incidents followed, including the terrible events of the Peterloo Massacre in August 1819 when several people were killed and about seventy injured when the 15th Hussars were ordered to charge into a crowd in Manchester — an event still in the minds of many who witnessed the opening of the Liverpool and Manchester Railway eleven years later.

From 1819, a bleak year for the nation in both human and economic terms, matters began slowly to improve. A growth period of six years to a prosperity peak in 1825 was to be the beginning of a series of boom and depression cycles which became a hallmark of the British economy, but the business interests of the time knew nothing of this syndrome and saw only the opportunity for expansion and profit. The conditions were right for the birth of Britain's railway system.

The Stockton and Darlington Railway was born of an increase in the demand for coal, the mineral foundation of Britain's greatness and the key to so much change in the nineteenth century. To keep pace with the needs of London and the manufacturing centres better facilities were needed to get Durham coal to the coast. Right from 1810 there were rival schemes and routes but the locomotive work on Tyneside of men like Chapman, Hedley and Stephenson was beginning to be noticed and the decision between the alternative canal, canal plus railway and railway options was taken in favour of the latter at a fateful meeting at Darlington in 1818. With no great war, depression or unrest to hold up its progress, this pioneer railway was duly opened on 27 September 1825.

The origins of that other great railway pioneer, the Liverpool and Manchester Railway, show an even closer connection with the changes in the affairs of the nation. Lancashire had expanded rapidly from the middle of the eighteenth century until towns like Manchester, Bolton and Bury had become great manufacturing centres for cotton goods, fed by the neighbouring coalfields, using water from the slopes of the Pennines and demanding every available roadway and waterway for the movement of their supplies and products. Cotton and iron goods from East Lancashire, plus salt from neighbouring Cheshire, passed to Liverpool for export and the port there, facing the growing colonies across the Atlantic, had expanded at a phenomenal rate. The process continued into the nineteenth century with Manchester doubling in size and Liverpool recording a 128 per cent increase in the number of vessels berthing between 1800 and 1825.

This growth in the Liverpool and Manchester areas put tremendous pressure on the road and waterway systems linking the two. The turnpike route, following much of the present A57 road, was described as 'circuitous, crooked and rough' and the average coach speeds of 12mph were only achieved by some hair raising driving producing, in turn, some highly uncomfortable journeys. Three changes of horses took place along the way so that to achieve an average of 12mph meant driving at 20mph or more wherever there was a gap between the plodding pack horses and lumbering freight wagons and when the private carriages of the gentry could be persuaded to give ground.

Although coaches were used by the business fraternity, the bulk movement of goods between Lancashire's two major towns was mainly by waterway using either the Mersey and Irwell Navigation, the Bridgewater Canal or the roundabout route of the Leeds and Liverpool Canal which opened a link from Wigan to Leigh specifically for this business in 1821. The limited capacity of the road system and the circuitous route of the Leeds and Liverpool Canal put the Mersey and Irwell, and Bridgewater enterprises in an enviable position which they exploited in concert and to the full. These two routes alone had the capacity to meet the needs of the vigorous industry and enterprise of the region and they priced accordingly. The rate for cotton became as high as twenty shillings a ton and even the formation of private carrying companies was not capable of producing a significant reduction in this figure for the canal owning interests successfully blocked attempts to develop independent warehousing along their waterways.

This situation produced for the Duke of Bridgewater and his estate a return on the original construction capital of around 40 per cent annually, and anything likely to jeopardise this comfortable position was viewed with considerable disfavour. Yet, at the same time, the trade interests were becoming more and more dissatisfied, not only by the high rates but also by the indifferent service. The sheer volume of the traffic to be moved meant considerable delays in waiting for boats, wharves or passage and, since the two shorter routes were both approached via the Mersey estuary and affected by its tides, there were frequent water shortages in summer either at the Liverpool end awaiting high tide or due to drought at the upstream end. Winter was little better for ice could close the waterways for days on end, while the constant thieving and damage completed the process of adding the insult of poor service to the injury of high rates.

In 1822 the Liverpool interests behind the projected new railway persuaded the Liverpool Corn Exchange to ask the Bridgewater Trust for some easement of its canal tolls, but the latter's superintendent replied that 'having taken into full consideration the allegations . . . and all the information he is in possession of on the subject, he does not feel justified in making any alteration.' Less than two years later when the railway's subscription list was nearly full, the canal charges were cut substantially! Even before it was built, the Liverpool and Manchester Railway was starting to make an impact on its community.

The years between 1820 and 1830 witnessed not only the emergence of the first significant railway schemes but also growing dissatisfaction with the old system of Parliamentary representation. Boroughs which had diminished in importance continued to send members to Parliament while places like Manchester, Leeds and Birmingham, the very growth centres of the nation's industrial activity, were not represented. Most of the 'rotten boroughs' were in the hands of the great landowners who traded them as they saw fit and Members who had bought such seats frequently recouped their outlay by selling their votes to the highest bidder. In this matter the reformers, led by Burdett and supported by the Whigs, were the champions of the middle classes, just the same men who sought to free their trade from the stranglehold of the privileged classes, especially as represented by the Bridgewater Trust's canal interests and similar constraints upon the growth of commerce and the exercise of enterprise. Railways became a factor in the challenge to the old order and an essential factor in the new; as *The Times* quoted later, 'The Nineteenth Century — Reform Bill passed. Steam engines, railways, penny postage, steam navigation, friction matches, telegraphs . . . O Wondrous Age.'

Localised and modestly reported as the first railway schemes were, they soon began to make an impact, first in their own areas and then upon other localities, trades and interests. They drew support from those who saw the advantages of better communications or the opportunity for profitable investment or land sale, and were bitterly opposed by coach operators, road and canal carriers, canal

'Juvenile Surveyors at Work' – a cartoon reflecting the growth in railway schemes

owners and even shipping companies, for many early journeys involved river or coastal vessels. The size of the two camps was increased by the likely effect of changes which railways would inevitably bring. Landowners wanted no intrusion upon their estates, inn keepers worried about fewer coach passengers to feed and re-horse, and clergymen were concerned about the impact of trains and the wider world they would offer upon the souls of their parishioners. The attitudes spread even further with employees taking the line of their employers, cranks warning of countless dangers to health and limb, political parties supporting rival schemes and those without jobs scenting the hope of fresh employment.

These early attitudes towards railways, developing only slowly because of the limited information available via pamphlets, limited circulation magazines and such newspapers as there were, were liable to distortion for the printed word circulated largely among those likely to be biased by their own position anyway while others received their news second or third hand. *The Times* might write about 'the immense benefits to be derived from the construction of new railways' but this was unlikely to have consoled the Liverpool and Manchester Railway supporters for the loss of their 1825 Bill or to have modified the hardcore opposition which was to re-appear for the 1826 Session. This was a period when many were consumed by their own causes and such public opinion as there was tended, as in all ages, to favour avoiding the discomfort of change. For every one convinced of the value of the new railway schemes there was an extremist who saw only a vision of passengers maimed or suffocated, horses bolting and vegetables refusing to grow.

For the early railways there could be no plans, estimates or submission to Parliament without a survey and this is where the opposing attitudes first began to harden. Creevey had a vision of 'the loco-motive Monster carrying *eighty tons* of goods and navigated by a tail of smoke and sulphur, coming thro' every man's grounds between Manchester and Liverpool', and many feared that radicals and dissenters would stream out from the towns into their strongholds in rural England. They showed their fears in opposition to the survey teams, already something of a problem for railways for there were few who could do such work effectively and those who could became in such demand that they took on too much work and risked illness or mistakes.

In the efforts of William James to survey the route of the Liverpool and Manchester Railway he found that these fears and attitudes had hardened into physical opposition. After having earlier given a preliminary opinion on the route, James began in 1822 a more detailed survey using a team of six assistants, one of whom was the young Robert Stephenson, fresh from Edinburgh College. Most of the landowners would not allow the survey team on their property and this antagonism spread through tenants and farm workers to the local populace who barracked and pelted the unfortunate surveyors. Samuel Smiles records that James engaged a prize fighter to carry the theodolite and that he became involved in a fierce fight with a St Helens miner. The professional won but the miner's friends routed the rest of the survey team with stones and destroyed the offending theodolite.

Although James had planned his route so as to avoid the most sensitive areas of private land, not to cross the principal roads and to give more than adequate waterway clearances, this failed to mollify the opposition. Matters were no better for George Stephenson's 1824 survey. He encountered more stone throwing and abuse, and this time firearms were added to the hazards. The estate staff fired guns at night to prevent the survey being carried out under cover of darkness and the survey teams countered this by their own ruse of firing guns to lure the estate workers away from the places they really intended to examine. There was very tangible expression of the way in which the rich feared for their privacy, their farming and their hunting. They convinced their tenants and workers that if the trains came they would destroy their crops by fire and their livestock by fear — all partly true, of course, for lineside crop fires were common enough in later years and many an unfortunate animal has strayed onto a railway line and met an unpleasant end.

Life was pretty hard upon those seeking to promote the early railways. In addition to the physical opposition encountered by James and Stephenson there were usually time pressures as well. If a Parliamentary session was missed a rival scheme might appear or capital be diverted to other projects. Stephenson was under a great deal of time pressure to enable the L&M to submit a petition for a Bill in the 1825 session and Brunel experienced a similar situation before the submission of the first Great Western Railway Bill in 1834.

To meet his deadlines, Brunel had to complete his survey between March and May 1833. He achieved this but only at the expense of days which started at first light, were filled with a hectic round of journeying and directing his assistants, and ended with late night meetings or the writing of notes by the light of some guttering hotel candle. That his judgement was sound history has proved and Brunel's diaries make it clear that this was no accident, for the tunnel through Box Hill was not chosen without seeing and rejecting the 'rotten oolite laying on clay' in the Avon valley and the line of the railway at Goring was chosen by taking the trouble to climb all the way to the top of 'the high hill south of Streatley'. In the process of all this journeying the railway surveyors helped to spread the news of the new enterprise so that few along the line of route could avoid taking up a position for or against the advent of the new railway.

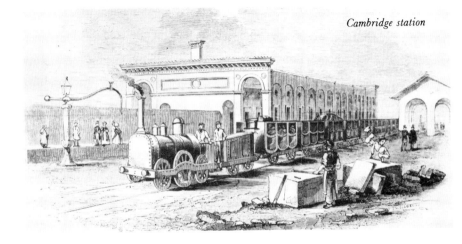

Cambridge station

After the years of unrest in Britain's home and foreign affairs a period of stability at the beginning of the 1820s stimulated the economy and made investors eager for profitable opportunities. The inadequacies of the existing transport facilities made it inevitable that several railway schemes, such as the Birmingham and Liverpool Railroad Company, should figure in the wave of speculation that ultimately swept the stock market. More railway projects figured in the second wave of promotion between 1836 and 1837 and then, in the period 1844-7, came the phenomenon labelled as the 'Railway Mania' when hundreds of schemes were lodged with Parliament in a frenzy of development which added many miles to the railway network but ruined thousands in the process.

The process of launching a railway project was a long and complicated one and attitudes for and against the scheme hardened as the process unfolded. While the new line was just talk at public meetings the matter could be treated lightly but as the promoters gathered 'big names' to endorse their cause and the issue of a prospectus gave it substance those who feared the effects of the new line began to consider how they might thwart its plans. Following the survey, and given a satisfactory response to the subscription list, a Parliamentary agent would be appointed and a 'Parliamentary Notice' published. Since this had to specify the route all now knew exactly what was planned and would react accordingly.

As railways grew wise in the ways of promoting their schemes they learned to avoid as much of the opposition as possible. After the defeat of the first Liverpool and Manchester Bill the revised route prepared by Vignoles left Liverpool well south of the first Stephenson line to limit the impact on Lord Derby's estates at Knowsley and avoid altogether the property of Lord Sefton. But the first promoters had little except the canal legislation to guide them and frequently learned the hard way. In some cases the opposition could be dealt with by compromise and the railway running and maintenance costs of later years were to be significantly affected by the tunnels, deviations, clearances and private stations or special stop arrangements demanded as the price for the right of passage of the line. One of many cases was that of Squire Robert Gordon of Kemble who successfully negotiated for a tunnel where the Great Western & Cheltenham Union line passed his Kemble House and forced the location of the original Kemble station to a point beyond his lands and a mile north of its present position.

The formal preparation of a railway scheme for the Parliamentary process included drafting the Bill, compiling a 'Book of Reference' of the properties which would be affected by the new line, and preparing the 'Deposited Plan' which contained the physical details of the route. In addition to laying these items before Parliament, the information had also to be provided to each county Clerk of the Peace and to each parish council. Not infrequently, especially as the pace of promotion increased, prospectuses were more lurid than factual, the surveys perfunctory and routes sometimes drawn with a laughable disregard for the actual terrain through which the proposed railway was to pass.

By House of Commons Standing Orders, derived from the experience with authorising the canals, the Parliamentary Agent for the aspiring railway had a number of other duties and a good agent could make a world of difference to the chances of success. Acceptance of a petition for a railway Bill was conditional upon the deposit in the Private Bill Office of the plan, section and Book of Reference of the line, of a schedule of the affected landowners and tenants, and of details of the expected costs of construction and how they were to be funded. To the committee appointed to examine the petition the Parliamentary Agent had to furnish proof that local authorities had been advised of the railway scheme, that the intention to petition for a Bill had been published in specified newspapers, that the estimate of expenses had been certified and that a satisfactory subscription list had been prepared.

In addition to the formal processes of the petition for a railway Bill, much informal discussion and negotiation took place. As far as possible objections were accommodated and much lobbying took place of Members of Parliament and of others who might influence the course of events either directly or indirectly. Evidence was gathered, petitions and other favourable support was solicited and witnesses were lined up, both from the railway camp and from the trades and communities it would affect. However, after all the discussions had taken place and the preparation work completed, a hardcore of factions for and against the project remained, who had to battle it out in Parliament.

The first Liverpool & Manchester Bill was supported by no fewer than seventeen trade petitions and when it came up for the second reading had the backing of such leading figures as the Liverpool MPs William Huskisson and General Gascoyne. Its opponents failed to defeat the scheme at this stage and began to present their petitions opposing the measure. Eventually these totalled well over a hundred representations, mainly from landowners and the canal interests, but with a sprinkling of clerics and private individuals who feared disruption of the habits of their society or the morals of society in general.

In the end, after a marathon of presentation, cross-examination and discussion continuing from 21 March to 1 June 1825, the vote on the preamble to the Bill and its initial clauses went against the L&M party and the measure was withdrawn. The reasons were complex: inadequacies in the documents and plans, a poor and ill-prepared showing by George Stephenson, defects in the Parliamentary system itself and, not least, a fierce and well-organised opposition. Three other railway schemes, including the Brighton line, foundered in the same session but the railway promoters were too enterprising a breed to accept the reverses as more than just a delay to their plans.

When the Liverpool and Manchester Railway went to Parliament again, in the following year, it had learned the lessons of the 1825 defeat well. John Rennie had been appointed in place of George Stephenson and had commissioned the Vignoles survey, the revised route of which greatly reduced the opposition from landowners. A number of meetings had been held to ensure that the support in Parliament was better organised and a major opponent from the canal group, the Marquess of Stafford, had been persuaded to become a shareholder — to the tune of nearly a quarter of the issue! The opposition also relied overmuch on its alleged ability to meet the transport needs of the area, and finally lost the battle when the Bill received the Royal Assent on 5 May 1826.

After conquering the formidable tunnel approach to Liverpool and the perils of Chat Moss bog, the Liverpool and Manchester Railway opened in 1830. Several other local lines were already being developed and as success came to the new railways from London to Birmingham, Bristol and Southampton the whole concept began to attract more and more attention. For a while lines still encountered opposition from special interests. The GWR, for example, had its share in the shape of the antagonism from the authorities of Eton College and the University governing body at Oxford, but in both cases good sense ultimately prevailed and the railway was admitted — subject to powers granted to the educational hierarchy to enter railway property in the pursuit of wayward scholars! For the second half of 1831 the L&M declared a dividend of $4\frac{1}{2}$ per cent and for the first time the financial expectations held out by railway proprietors became a firm reality and began to influence attitudes. By the end of the decade

An impression of the scene outside the Board of Trade on the night of Sunday 30 November 1845 and depicting the scramble to deposit Bills before the deadline

dividends of £4 8s 9d from the London and Birmingham Railway, £1 10s 0d from the Great Western Railway and £3 10s 0d from the York and North Midland Railway were on offer.

Gradually the public interest quickened. The opposition to new schemes began to come more from rival railways than from protectionist groups and a new age of railway intrigue dawned. Soon the main worry of investors was which scheme to support, whether its promoters were honest and whether their project would triumph over its rivals rather than whether to support a railway scheme at all.

Inevitably the pendulum of interest and support swung too far. It was fortuitous that the success of the early railways should become increasingly apparent at a time when national pressure for the repeal of restrictive measures was growing and should coincide with an appetite for expansion and reform. The Corn Law of 1815 prohibited the importation of grain while the home selling price was less than £16 per cwt, but the nation's workforce needed cheaper bread to avoid going hungry and employers saw a lower cost of living as a factor in containing wage bills. Peel responded to these pressures in his 1841-6 ministry with an 1842 budget which cut duties on raw materials and with successive further easements culminating in the repeal of the Corn Law in 1846. His 'free trade' principles, intended 'to make this country a cheap country for living', stimulated a great deal of development, not least in the demand for transport.

The first railway boom produced schemes estimated to cost over £20m but the great mania of 1845-7 involved amounts of ten times this figure, with hundreds of competing projects in existence and involving over 20,000 route miles. In the end less than half this mileage was authorised, but not before every class of society had been involved in the mad scramble to promote schemes, deposit plans and launch subscription lists.

Since the railway subscription lists called only for a signature or modest

The opening of the Leamington-Warwick line in 1844 with a few 'well-dressed spectators' gathered to see the opening train at Kenilworth station

deposit it was easy to speculate. Everyone did so, men of trade shrewdly, men of fashion much as they would have wagered on a horse, old maids believing it would make their remaining years secure and young girls seeing the anticipated dividends as a golden dowry to enhance their prospects of a suitable marriage. But matters were very different when the costs of the Parliamentary marathon began to mount up and when the construction costs made the share calls more frequent and for larger sums. This was the first indication to the over-eager investor of the hard facts of his commitment but in the unreal interval before this happened subscription signatures seemed easy to come by, everyone believed they would get rich as a railway shareholder and the sum involved in the 620 new railway projects counted by *The Times* at the end of 1845 rose to a staggering £563m — and at least as many more schemes had still to register their prospectuses.

These Railway Mania years influenced the country as a whole and not just the railway promoter and investor. The availability of investment capital not only inflated the value of railway shares but affected things like land prices which rose sharply at the slightest hint of a railway scheme. As construction work began the cost of materials tended to rise and higher wages would frequently be paid in an effort to shorten the costly interval between the beginning of the project and the time when traffic would begin to flow and produce some income. These higher wages, in turn, affected those in other employment and the general availability of labour.

As always, *Punch* mirrored the absurd side of the situation. It envisaged an extension of the 'Births, Marriages and Deaths' columns of the newspapers to allow readers to keep abreast of the progress of railway schemes. and a railway cemetery was suggested as a place for disappointed attorneys, engineers, scrip-holders and committee men to grieve. There had been thoughts of an 'Asylum for Railway Lunatics' to house those proposing useless schemes and *Punch* later worried about the injunction granted to prevent railway shares being sold to a lunatic. 'This sets a fearful precedent', it warned. 'How many of the transactions of the railway mania will be allowed to stand?'

Another form of comment on the more farcical aspects of the boom was the offer of prospectuses from mythical companies. One such suggested by a waspish writer with no mean imagination was that of the 'Grand Antipodean and Hemispherical Junction Railway'. This was to run between Glasgow and Sydney by a 'straight line through the centre of the earth' with gravity playing a large part in the traction plans and the movement of gold from Golconda to Glasgow ensuring the line's traffic prosperity!

The 'unhealthy state of fever', as Brunel saw the mania years, could not continue. So much theoretical money was in circulation that the Bank of England was forced to raise the bank rate in 1846 to restrain the movement of gold and credit. Shares tumbled, many schemes failed completely and many a pound invested achieved no more than to contribute to the costs of promoting a line. Instead of solving the investor's financial problems by fulfilling his dreams the effect of railways upon the life of the community now became as likely to be a disaster as a financial miracle worker.

Fortunately the earlier and better schemes survived the dramatic changes in

The construction achievement is well dramatised in this engraving of the first Folkestone train passing through Bletchingley Tunnel on 24 June 1843

the market place for capital. The new mileage authorised fell from a peak of 4,541 in 1846 to 373 miles in 1848 and only 7 in 1850 but the mileage opened was still 621 in the latter year. The existing railways cut back on their expansion plans as shareholders imposed constraints on the capital account, but many lines were caught part completed by the diminishing supply of money and had either to find further sources of cash or abandon the investment already made. With the ingenuity which marked the period, ways were usually found, including the tactic of recycling money already invested by increasing investment or participation by the contractors who had done well out of the building process. Slowly things picked up, lines were completed and the cycle of more facilities, more traffic, more demand was soon to be producing more mini booms in this buoyant period of the railways' history.

Although so many saw their savings lost or reduced in value by the worst aspects of the railway promotion periods, the railway route mileage increased by 4,600 miles in the 1840s and whole trades and communities shared in the benefits of the construction activity. Few lines were built within their original estimates but this hardly worried the quarry owners, the suppliers of tools, bricks, timber and mortar, and others in trades as diverse as horse breeder and iron founder. Thousands were able to draw a regular, if hard-earned, wage from their construction labours and the people involved included not only the navvies, but also the craftsmen — smiths, masons, carpenters and bricklayers — and the professionals — solicitors, surveyors, engineers and accountants.

In addition to its effects locally, railway construction came to alter the lives of the community as a whole. Brunel was unable to get enough masons locally to meet his needs for bridges, tunnels and buildings on the Bristol to Chippenham section of the Great Western route. Accordingly he instructed his agent in the north to try to recruit 150-200 masons in the Edinburgh and Glasgow areas by offering them six months employment with travel expenses paid and with wages varying between 3s 6d and 4s 6d per day. When this failed to produce the required results the top wage rate on offer was increased by 3d and the recruitment area extended to Aberdeen.

Excavation by steam power made no real impact on the construction industry until the last years of the nineteenth century so the mammoth process of digging railway cuttings, building up embankments and boring tunnels was largely a manual one. Using tub wagons on contractors' lines, horses trained to dodge the tipping of the wagon and with some measure of pulleys, sheer legs and gins, the railway labourers would shift anything up to 20 tons a day each and average three shillings for their pains. They might have little opportunity to spend this other than in the contractor's 'tommy shop' but spend it they did and the economic cycle of consumption and production proceeded a little faster as a result. Some of the navvies came from building canals, others deserted farms and similar employment to become 7s 6d a week better off, but despite the repercussions of these changes the total number of jobs available was increased, fewer needed to seek relief or go hungry, related activities prospered and many who lost labour were forced, to their ultimate benefit, to find more efficient methods of working.

At last the agonies of promoting a railway scheme and the disruption of building the line came to an end, culminating in what became another railway institution, the opening day celebration. There was some demonstration against the opening of the Liverpool and Manchester line at the Manchester end but this was directed more at the Duke of Wellington than at the railway. Magnificent as a military campaigner, the Duke was not successful as a politician, seeing little need for popular support for his policies, averse to change in home affairs and inflexible in his foreign attitudes. The general reaction to the opening of new lines was favourable, some seeing the benefits that better transport would bestow, others just glad of a spectacle that would brighten lives overfilled with work and offering little in the way of entertainment beyond fairs, religious festivals and the alehouse. Whatever the individual motives, Liverpool was full by the day preceding the opening of the Liverpool and Manchester and enterprising businessmen were offering accommodation, seats in the special trains, room in one of the various viewing stands erected along the route and a choice of a range of souvenirs. Commerce was beginning to taste some of the side benefits of the railway enterprise.

Ten years after the opening of the Liverpool to Manchester line the North Midland Railway enterprise celebrated its opening on 5 July 1840. The *Sheffield and Rotherham Independent* commented:

> The completion of this vast undertaking, which has at last made Yorkshire a sharer in the great advantages of railway communication that Lancashire has for some years enjoyed, is no ordinary event.
>
> It opens to a million and a half Yorkshiremen a mode of communication with the Midland Counties and the metropolis, such as twenty years ago would have been ridiculed as a Utopian chimera, being actually equivalent in time to a reduction of the distance by two thirds.

Interior of the Midland Counties Railway station at Derby, 1843

The opening of Crewe Works

The formal opening had taken place on Tuesday 30 June when 600 people had been invited to attend. The special train left Sheffield at 9.30am and waited at Masborough for the train from Leeds which duly arrived at 10.30am. Drawn by two engines and pushed by a third, this train 'appeared to be of interminable length' but despite this the Sheffield coaches were added and the mammoth set off for Derby. In the manner of such events, at Derby station — 'one of the wonders of the railway system' — there awaited tables 'covered with an almost unbounded variety of substantial and elegant viands.' With a frank comment on human nature, the reporter continues, 'Upon these the guests fell with undisguised satisfaction, and but a short time was spent in making an ample and most grateful report.' Despite this feasting at Derby the occupants of the 48-coach train managed another substantial meal at Leeds when they returned there and happily toasted the royal family, local worthies and the armed forces. The band of the 4th Royal Irish Dragoons made sure that no one slept off their over-indulgence and by the time the Sheffield contingent set off for home at 11pm they must have felt that it had been quite a full day.

Some of the contemporary attitudes, hopes and fears showed through the reporting. 'We used to hear it said that railway travelling would deprive passengers of the opportunity of observing the scenery, as they would be whirled over the country too rapidly to look about them,' comments the newspaper, but explains that the eye can keep distant sights in view for sufficient time to enjoy them and that embankments make admirable viewing elevations. The traveller gets, it concludes from the opening day experience, 'a far more enlarged view of the character of the country than he can from those slower methods of travelling in which the tedium, the weariness and the annoyances of the journey, wear out attention.'

The fear that horses would bolt at the sight of a train was commonplace. It too shows up in the reporting of the North Midland Railway opening day special when four horses wandered onto an embankment between Barnsley and Wakefield. 'The engineer slackened his speed, and sounded the most prolonged and dismal screech that ever astonished our ears,' said the newspaper description, adding the news that the chastened animals galloped away none the worse for their experience. So much for the claim made to the Eastern Counties Railway relating to 'a horse drove into the river and so much drowned as never stood any more' or the cows 'drove from their lodging and sadly disturbed'.

The thoughtful view saw all benefiting from the new lines springing up around the country. It was summed up in one of the speeches on the North Midland Railway's opening day, when the speaker felt sure 'that every class of society felt the benefit of a railway — the capitalist found his money brought into profitable employment; the professional man, the manufacturer, the mechanic, the labourer were all employed, and the merchant and landowner reaped great advantage.'

Prior to the advent of railways very few people travelled and even fewer did so in any degree of comfort. It is not surprising, therefore, that the novelty of the early railway travel shows up in the reporting it received. On the inaugural North Midland journey mentioned in the last chapter the *Sheffield and Rotherham Independent* reporter recorded his impressions in detail. Of Clay Cross Tunnel — another wonder, except to the few who might have passed through a canal tunnel — he observed:

> Numerous shafts pass through the hill upward, but the depth is so great, that as to lighting the tunnel, they have little more effect than to shed a circle of dungeon light upon the ground immediately beneath them. The air of the tunnel is, of course, somewhat damp, chilly and sulphurous, but not so much as to be peculiarly disagreeable. In the roofs of the first class carriages, a lamp burns, but in the second class the darkness is entire . . . . Nothing can be seen except . . . the hot cinders which drop from the engines, and look like lines of fire upon the ground.

Derby station is recorded as 'one of the wonders of the railway system' and the description of the engine house there revealed just how clearly the locomotive

An early 0-6-0 locomotive built in 1855 for the Oxford, Worcester and Wolverhampton Railway showing the almost non-existent weather protection for the bearded driver. This railway was absorbed by the West Midland in 1860 and then by the GWR three years later

was seen as a successor to the horse:

> It is a polygon of sixteen sides, and 130ft in diameter, lighted from a dome-shaped roof of the height of 53ft. It contains sixteen lines of rails, radiating from a single turn-table in the centre; the engines, upon their arrival, will be brought in here, placed upon the turn-table, and wheeled into any stall that may be vacant. Each of the sixteen stalls in these locomotive engine stables will hold two, or perhaps three engines; and here the iron-horses will receive every attention after they have been fatigued and harassed by their work.

A more objective impression of the early lines is provided by an account of a journey from Liverpool to Manchester in 1831. The writer was Colonel Pownoll Phipps of the Hon East India Company who recorded the new experience in his diary for 5 April 1831:

> April 5. After partaking of a hasty breakfast, I got, at seven o'clock, on the celebrated railway, and found myself at Liverpool in an hour and a half. An omnibus took up the passengers with their luggage at the office in the town of Manchester, and conveyed them to the outskirts where the railway begins, and on the Liverpool side there are similar conveyances ready to carry them near the Town Hall. I observed that one small locomotive engine, with a car of coals behind, was fastened to six carriages each having three bodies holding six persons; the seats divided by small bars. They are regularly numbered, and the ticket delivered at the office for five shillings shows the seat to which you are entitled. Thus all confusion is avoided. The ends of the carriages have strong leather mufflers to soften the force of the blow when they come in contact with each other, which frequently occurs when the engine stops. We stopped for water at a half-way house, and once to regulate something out of order. The speed was by no means uniform, but varied considerably. At every mile a watchman is stationed to keep the way clear from stones, and to prevent any tricks being played to injure the railway. We first passed on the road a string of carriages like our own, coming from Liverpool. The velocity with which both bodies are moving, separated only by a space of two or three feet, gave a terrific appearance to this occurrence, although, in reality there is no danger when each person keeps his seat, and does not put the head out of the window. We next passed, in the same manner, some open cars, the price of a seat in which is only two shillings and six pence; but passengers are exposed to inconvenience from the steam, and in the winter they must be very cold, going so rapidly through the air. The last carriages we passed were platforms laden with merchandise and poultry. A gentleman's carriage was conveyed across on one of these platforms.
> On arriving at a tunnel near Liverpool the steam-carriage was taken off, and the coaches slowly moved under the rocky arch by ropes turned by steam, and on clearing the dark passage, omnibuses were in readiness to convey the passengers to their inns. No fees of any description are taken, and the whole is very well managed. Two hundred tons of cotton had recently been conveyed across in one trip by two locomotive engines, in two hours and a half, the charge for which was one hundred pounds, or about a farthing for conveying four pounds and a half of cotton thirty one miles.

Travelling

BY THE

RAILWAY.

THE DIRECTORS of the LIVERPOOL and MANCHESTER RAILWAY beg leave to inform the Public, that on and after MONDAY next the 4th of October, the Railway Coaches will start from the Stations in Liverpool and Manchester respectively, at the following hours:—

The FIRST CLASS COACHES, Fare 7s.
At Seven o'Clock.
Ten o'Clock.
One o'Clock.
Half-past Four o'Clock.

The SECOND CLASS COACHES, Fare 4s.
At Eight o'Clock.
Two o'clock.

On Sundays, the First Class Coaches will start at Seven o'Clock in the Morning, and half-past Four in the Afternoon ; and the Second Class Coaches at half-past Six in the Morning, and Four in the Afternoon.

Places may be booked at the Liverpool end, either at the Station in Crown-street, or at the Company's Coach Office, in Dale-street ; and at the Manchester end at the Coach Office in Liverpool-road, or at the Company's Coach Office in Market-street, corner of New Cannon-street, where Plans of the Coaches constituting each Train will lie, in order that Passengers may make choice of their respective Seats. Tickets for which will be given on payment of the Fare.

A conveyance by Omnibusses twenty minutes before each of the above-mentioned hours of departure of the First Class Coaches only, will proceed from the Company's Office, Dale-street, to Crown-street, free of charge, for Sixty-eight Passengers and their Luggage. (the said number, *first booked*, having the preference, on their claiming it at the time of booking) and for the same number *from* Crown-street to Dale-street, on the arrival of the Coaches from Manchester, a preference on the same terms being given to Passengers first booked at the Company's Coach Offices, Manchester.

After the Festival week, during which it is impossible to ensure the desired accommodation, a conveyance to and from Crown-street will be provided for all the Passengers carried by the First Class Coaches.

Parcels will be received at any of the Company's Coach Offices, and delivered with the greatest regularity at the usual rates, and without any charge for booking or delivering.

No fee or gratuity is allowed to be taken by any Porter, Guard, Engine-man, or other servant of the Company, and the Directors are determined to enforce this regulation by the immediate dismissal of any person in their employ offending against it.

Railway Office, John-street, Liverpool, 30th *September,* 1830.

PRINTED BY BANCKS AND CO. EXCHANGE STREET.

Reprint 1930.

The early arrangements and regulations of the Liverpool and Manchester Railway

The Phipps account gives some idea of just how much the Liverpool and Manchester Railway had achieved, not just in building its line but also in devising safe and efficient operating practices and in planning its traffic facilities and systems. It had little in the way of precedent to go on. Indeed, the ideas taken from stage coach practice soon became an embarrassment and the requirement to book tickets 24 hours in advance, for example, had been replaced by the issue of hand written tickets 'on demand' by 1831.

One of the Liverpool and Manchester's early difficulties was that passengers brought their stage coach habits with them. Punctuality was no new discipline since both mail and stage coaches tried hard to maintain good timekeeping, but patrons of wealth and position took some convincing that trains should not wait for them as their own coachman would do, and the sheer numbers using the new mode of travel was an unprecedented experience. A number of early passengers thought that they could ride outside a railway coach or jump off before it had come to a stop and several early accidents derived from such factors. Another major difficulty was that stops on a road journey signalled the opportunity for the passengers to stretch their legs and take refreshment, and for the local tradesmen to sell them something, and both groups took some convincing that a railway journey could not be treated in the same way.

The seven shillings paid by the early first class traveller on the Liverpool and Manchester Railway covered not only his train journey, but also the omnibus between the company's town office in Dale Street, Liverpool and the Crown Street station there. He not only need pay no more but was actually dissuaded from doing so by the railway's handbills which stated:

> No fee or gratuity is allowed to be taken by any Porter, Guard, Engine-man, or other servant of the Company, and the Directors are determined to enforce this regulation by the immediate dismissal of any person in their employ offending against it.

This must have been hard to accept by those used to stage coach ways where the lower fares went to the coachman and guard as part of their remuneration and extra payments were essential if the traveller was to enjoy a comfortable seat, safe

Interior of the Great Western terminus at Paddington showing the Great Western Railway's 'better class of passenger'

This well-known engraving shows early Liverpool and Manchester Railway passenger and freight trains. The first-class carriages (top) were constructed in the form of three stage coach bodies to produce one carriage. Each carriage was named in a similar manner to stage coaches. The guard rode on the top of the front carriage and directed the engine driver, while the Royal Mail man guarded the mail box at the

rear. Second and third-class carriages were much more basic, with no weather protection at all. The goods and cattle wagons (bottom) were provided by the carriers, not the railway company, whose men travelled freely with the goods as when carting upon public roads

stowage of his luggage and decent food and accommodation on the journey. Not to have need of refreshment on a journey also took some getting used to and the habit of taking food along persisted even though the journey time might now hardly warrant it.

The view of the early railways seems to have been that there would be no demand for travel other than from those classes of person already in the habit of making journeys. As late as 1839 in evidence before a committee of Parliament it was clear that the Great Western Railway had not really thought about facilities for third class passengers although it should have occurred to them that if goods were to go by train, there would also be a demand from those who could only afford to travel in the slow, lumbering stage wagons with the goods. Lines like the London and Croydon Railway and the Grand Junction Railway initially made no provision for 'the very lowest orders of passengers', as Charles Saunders of the Great Western had described them, although the London and Birmingham took an interest right from opening its first section in 1837 and advertised 'Third class coaches carry four passengers on each seat and are without covering.'

When the Great Western did change its mind it referred to the new class of travellers as 'Goods Train Passengers' and clearly saw the association between such people and the movement of goods as continuing. It would convey them only in uncovered trucks, by goods train and usually at the most inconvenient of hours. Seated on low wooden boards in low sided wagons these third class passengers were very vulnerable and eight died on Christmas Eve 1841 when the 4.30am goods from Paddington ran into an earth slip in Sonning Cutting.

This incident was curious as well as tragic in that it invoked the old *deodand* law under which any object causing the death of a person was to be given to God. A

The hustle and bustle outside Paddington Station in 1843

payment of £1,000 was initially fixed as the price at which the Great Western Railway could redeem the deodandum engine and rolling stock involved, although this was subsequently reduced on appeal. One good thing coming out of the tragedy was that it led directly to the company increasing the height of the sides of its open trucks, and it may also have influenced the Bill for the Cheap Trains Act introduced in 1844 by Gladstone during Peel's ministry.

The 1844 legislation required railways to provide on all lines a service once a day for conveying third class passengers, in carriages protected from the elements, at fares not exceeding a penny per mile and at an average speed of not less than 12mph. Still fearing that cheap travel would diminish their profits and offend the better off travellers they carried, the railways complied more with the letter than the spirit of the new measure. In most cases the old open trucks were just replaced by closed trucks with shutters to admit air and light and comply with the Act's stipulations requiring illumination and ventilation. In some cases tarpaulins were provided instead, but what is today adequate to deal with a summer shower during the quaintness of a Vale of Rheidol journey would hardly have been reasonable for a four or five hour stopping train journey in the darkness of a cold, wet winter's evening in the 1840s. Skylights, plank seats and drainage holes in the floor to let out the rain were other refinements enjoyed by the third class passenger of the period.

◀ *The popular view of First Class Passengers*

▲
Second Class Passengers

▲
Third Class Passengers or, as the Great Western Railway put it 'the very lowest order of passengers'

While all this was going on the lot of the first and second class travellers steadily improved and the third and fourth classes were eventually to benefit as the railways began the habit of handing down coaches outmoded on the best services to those paying a lower fare or using inferior trains and lines. The earliest vehicles for first class travel consisted of three enclosed compartments in the stage coach tradition, each providing six passengers with armrests and upholstery, and the whole mounted on a four-wheel iron frame chassis. With no springing, little elasticity in the track and locomotive handling which had yet to become a skilled profession even these coaches must have been pretty uncomfortable. However, it was not long before simple springs and buffing gear were provided — Brunel favouring 'elastic hair' for stuffing the latter — and the gradual introduction of six-wheeled vehicles brought not only the addition of another compartment and more ornate fittings but also a reduction in the lateral 'hunting' motion occurring during the journey. Seating remained three a side in the first class accommodation, four in the second and, in the third and fourth classes, as many as could be crowded in. Distinctions of fare and status were maintained in all things. The luggage allowance enabled the well-to-do to take mountains of bags, rugs, portmanteaux and other items along, but the passenger in the open truck was allowed only 14lb. The primitive oil lamps were allocated on the basis of one per first class compartment, one between two second class compartments and often only one per coach or truck for the luckless third class user.

The spartan nature of the early railway accommodation led to the proferring of advice, both humourous and well-intentioned, for those bold enough to undertake a railway journey. In *The Iron Road Book*, published in 1838, Francis Coghlan described the railway route from London to Birmingham, Manchester and Liverpool and provided both details of its facilities and an account of the towns it served. He makes reassuring noises about safety — including a calculation that only 1/450th of the air in a tunnel would become contaminated even if the tunnel had no ventilating shaft — and refers to first class accommodation as having 'all the seats alike . . . comfortably fitted up'. But his advice to the users of second class carriages, 'or rather *wagons*', is less reassuring:

> In the first place, get as far from the engine as possible — for three reasons:-
> *First,* should an explosion take place, you may happily get off with the loss of
> an arm or a leg — whereas if you should happen to be placed near the said
> piece of hot machinery, and an unfortunate accident really occur, you would
> very probably be 'smashed to smithereens'. . . . *Secondly* — the vibration is very
> much diminished the further you are away from the engine. *Thirdly* — always
> sit (if you can get a seat) with your back towards the engine, against the
> boarded part of the wagon; by this plan you will avoid being chilled by a cold
> current of air which passes through these open wagons, and also save you from
> being nearly blinded by the small cinders which escape through the funnel.

For those not permanently put off rail travel by this well meaning advice, Coghlan goes on to give a factual picture of the process of taking any one of the seven trains then running northwards from Euston to Denbigh Hall or Birmingham:

> On driving into the yard on the left of the grand entrance, you are set down
> under a portico, from which admission is obtained to the pay departments, by
> separate doors, which are distinguished by having the name of the class
> painted on large lamps above the doors; thus rendering them serviceable both

at night and day. These doors are opened one hour before the starting of each train. Those persons who have booked their places at either of the offices mentioned elsewhere, merely show their ticket, and pass on either into the waiting-room or take their place in one of the carriages or wagons; those who are not booked elsewhere, pay their fare to the clerk, who gives a receipt ticket. On entering the interior of the station, strangers cannot but be struck with the novelty of the scene. The train destined for departure is drawn up alongside a raised stone platform, protected from the weather by a light handsome shed, supported by cast-iron pillars. To the carriages are affixed boards, with the names of the various towns to which passengers can proceed by coach from the railway stations — Oxford, Northampton, Banbury, & c. All passengers having taken their seats — on the striking of the clock, the office doors are shut, and the porters and police push the train about the distance of two hundred yards . . . the train is attached to a thick rope, worked by a steam engine. On a signal being given by a man stationed for the purpose, this is set in motion — and acting in the same manner that a line revolves round the wheel of a common lathe, draws the train up to the engine in three minutes . . . .

This little guide provides much supplementary information revealing, for example, that different colours were used for different classes of ticket (London used pink for first class and white for second, Birmingham yellow and blue) and that seat allocation had already started to give way to 'first come, first served'. It also notes the fares to Birmingham (£1 10s 0d first class, £1 second, only £1 17 0d for a two-wheel carriage, but 10s for a dog), records the routes of the omnibuses serving Euston and describes the system used for the coach and omnibus link which then filled the gap in the route pending the completion of the line between Denbigh Hall and Rugby. Parcels were already being carried by the railway, sleepers were anticipated by the ability to convert one compartment in the mail vehicles into a bed carriage and the trucks provided at all the principal stations for the conveyance of 'Gentlemens' Carriages' were surely part of the history of today's Motorail facility. But not all was convenient and praiseworthy. 'I could not help noticing,' warned Mr Coghlan diffidently, 'the awkwardness of many of the *green* porters — particularly at Rugby.'

Another aspect comes out of such early commentaries and gives a clue about the impact railways were already making. Coghlan talks about 12,000 men being employed on building the London and Birmingham Railway. Indeed, many such found a lifetime's work in building railways or the towns, factories and houses they stimulated, and by 1847 the railway industry was providing no less than 47,000 jobs directly and many more indirectly. Some of these, of course, only compensated for jobs lost in the old coaching and road trades, but the net gain was immense.

Our old friend the *Sheffield and Rotherham Independent* devoted some of its consideration of the new North Midland Railway to the sort of benefits it was likely to bring. Listing the approximate journey times to London (10 hours), Birmingham (4 hours), Leeds (1½ hours), York (2 hours) and Hull (4 hours), the newspaper observed, 'In communication with all these places, we may calculate upon the saving of two-thirds of the time, while the safety and pleasantness of travelling will be increased to an immense extent.'

Where an early writer in *John Bull* had feared that railways 'will give an unnatural impetus to society, destroy all the relations which exist between man and man, overthrow all mercantile regulations, overturn the metropolitan markets, drain the provinces of all their resources, and create, at the peril of life, all sorts of confusion and distress', the *Independent* dealt more in hard facts:

We find the letters which used to reach us from the south about two in the afternoon (and that was reckoned a great thing when first accomplished by the Halifax mail) are now ready for the earliest hours of business. The mail up, formerly despatched at night, for delivery the second morning after in London, now leaves us in the evening for delivery the next morning.

Once hand signals and time interval arrangements settled down, ground signals like this one began to appear

By the time the century reached its midway point over 6,000 miles of railway existed to facilitate the commerce and communication of the nation. The backbone of the network had been completed — including in 1850 itself the opening of the Britannia Bridge to establish the Royal Mail route to Holyhead, the completion of the London-Perth route, the South Wales Railway stretching west from Chepstow to Swansea, the completion of the East Coast route amalgam and the opening of the Royal Border Bridge.

By this time the tide of amalgamations was well under way. The Midland Railway had come into being in 1844 and the London and North Western Railway and the London, Brighton and South Coast Railway two years later. Semaphore signalling and the electric telegraph were in regular use, the Railway Clearing House was at work implementing the inter-company agreements and division of receipts, and the Gauge Commission had opted for 4ft 8½in even if the Great Western Railway's 256½ miles of 7ft gauge was to double before the 'narrow' gauge became 'standard'. In 1850 the railway system carried 73 million passengers and the value of freight traffic was soon to overtake that of the passenger business. Few lives were unaffected by the railway.

A POPULAR PASTIME
4

The second half of the nineteenth century began in style with the Great Exhibition of 1851. It was conceived 'to give the world a picture of the point of industrial development at which the whole of mankind has arrived and a new starting point for further exertions'. Altogether some six million people visited Joseph Paxton's great structure of glass and iron and the profits from the event were sufficient to allow the foundation of the South Kensington museum.

The success of the Great Exhibition owed much to the railway network without which it could not have drawn such large numbers of visitors but, in a way, it also did much in return to stimulate the growing excursion habit. The concept of providing special facilities for special events and at special fares dates right back to the days of the Liverpool and Manchester Railway, when the ceremonial coaches used on the opening day were made to earn their keep by conveying sightseers to see the Sankey viaduct. From 1840 the numbers of excursion trains operated began slowly to increase, with Thomas Cook running his first temperance excursion from Leicester to Loughborough (for a shilling, including refreshments and entertainment) on 5 July 1841 and expanding into pleasure trips four years later. Cook brought some 165,000 people to the 1851 exhibition and in the process introduced such concepts as saving up for the event through 'exhibition clubs' and the use of a travel magazine. He did a great deal of promotional work, touring the major towns with an advertising van, and also provided credit to help those who might have difficulty in raising the fare. Whereas most previous excursions had catered for groups with special interests — Sunday Schools, temperance societies and the like — Cook believed fervently that the working classes whose skill was on display in the exhibition products should have the facilities to witness the event. As a consequence many of those in the trains the Midland Railway despatched southwards to London were 'mechanics, artisans and other operative classes'.

This was an eventful period for Great Britain, with years of successive conflicts overseas accompanied by steady colonial development and of such progress at home that Chartism declined before the achievements of lower food prices and political reform and the steady improvements in social conditions and administration. There were many setbacks, like the Lancashire Cotton Famine which put half a million people on relief in 1862, but in the same period much of the sea carriage business of the North American states was acquired by Britain and by 1865 Gladstone was able to budget for a drop in income tax to fourpence in the pound!

The Eastern Counties Railway station at Peterborough as it was in 1845, an attractive building and a busy scene

In this atmosphere the railways thrived. In twenty years the freight business tripled and the number of passengers shot up to over 300 million annually. There was a change in the nature of the business too. The old concept of the 2d per mile of the first class passenger entitling him to the best and fastest accommodation and for 1d per mile the third class traveller having to accept an eleven-hour, all-stations journey from Euston to Liverpool had to go, for the nation's habits and social structure was changing as rapidly as its economic circumstances. In 1851, for example, the census revealed that for the first time there were more people living in the towns than in the countryside. Their consumption stimulated industrial demand and, less obvious but equally significant, produced changes in taste and habits. People wanted not only cheaper food but more variety, the middle classes began to take holidays and send their children to boarding schools, newspapers, theatres and music halls strove to cater for the entertainment appetites and society became progressively more sophisticated. As always, attitudes changed more slowly than events and many compromises had to be made so that the Lancashire and Yorkshire Railway, for example, in offering sea bathing excursions in the 1850s had to make it clear that those booking would be 'entitled to bathe and refresh themselves in ample time to attend a place of worship'.

More and more people wanted to make a railway journey, and they had little alternative for most of their journeys. But many were not used to the social mixing process that the event involved and some travellers, inevitably, would not prove the best of companions.

A traveller of 1848 gave pen to a complaint about 'drunkards and a madman' in the train he used. Despite making his journey on the Great Western, which still clung to its belief in encouraging only a better class of passenger, the traveller 'had not proceeded as far as Goring' before his delicate wife and three young children encountered 'extremely indecent and insulting conduct' from a drunken man and woman making the same journey. Our writer complained to the guard of the train who conducted him 'to a carriage wherein was a madman'. Not seeing this as an improvement in his circumstances, the luckless traveller alighted. 'Unless you get in the train will go without you,' threatened the guard. 'And so it did', records our unhappy passenger. But not far, for his protests halted the train into which he clambered back, finally resolving the matter by changing to a first class carriage at Didcot. Either this gentleman suffered from some form of persecution complex or local stations had already learned to pass on problems too difficult for them to handle for the letter writer concludes darkly: 'I have the address of a lady who saw him [the madman] forcibly put into the carriage at Reading.'

A few years after this Great Western Railway incident, a traveller on the London and South Western Railway experienced a different kind of drama. He was on the 1.10pm from Waterloo which had just passed Kingston when a companion spotted a lady clinging to the train outside the door of the adjoining compartment. With considerable courage and no little exertion our traveller, modestly signing the subsequent account only with the initials H.S., stretched out for the lady's hand and managed to draw her onto the footboard of his own compartment. The frightened female had already been sufficiently scared by the actions of a man in her compartment that she had opened the door in order to escape him, and she now fainted. With the train travelling at 40mph and a swooning damsel in his arms, her rescuer was in a situation worthy of the best drama writers. As he himself put it, 'I was compelled to hold her in this perilous position, with her dead weight on my arms, fast losing my own strength, while the train had travelled, I should think, at least five miles.' The ordeal ended happily when the guard spotted what was happening and stopped the train but, as H.S. concluded in his letter, 'I may add that when the lady fainted she slipped some inches, and had she touched the handle of the door you would not have received this letter from your obedient servant.'

Some of the novelty of railways and the part they played in everyday life is reflected in this habit of writing to the newspapers about railway matters. Such letters undoubtedly had some influence upon the railways' own striving after improvements, the subject of train communication being one that was receiving special attention at this period. A committee of the Railway Clearing House had studied the subject in 1852 and the matter received more prominence following the brutal murder of Thomas Briggs on a North London Railway train in 1864.

The London and South Western Railway already had some brake third vehicles with a raised roof for the guard's use, but this gave only limited visibility and would not have helped H.S. in his plight. Following the 1864 murder the London and South Western Railway provided circular holes in the compartment partitions in a bid to prevent the isolation which compartments represented being used for robbery and assault. The holes came to be known as Müller's Lights, after the man convicted of the North London Railway crime,

'Single driving wheel' locomotives were popular designs in the early Victorian era in an effort to raise running speeds. This Caledonian Railway 2-2-2 of 1861 originally had driving wheels of no less than 8ft 2in and no cab for the driver (the one shown here was added in 1869)

but they were not popular and did nothing to enable passengers to halt a train in an emergency. A more encouraging development came from the London and South Western Railway superintendent W.H. Preece who developed a simple electrical appliance for the job, although most companies responded to new requirements in the 1868 Regulation of Railways Act by providing an external cord connected to a gong or whistle on the engine.

The train on which H.S. was travelling probably stopped only because one of the enginemen looked back and saw something amiss. Fortunately most passenger coaches of the period had substantial grip rails alongside the door handles and the locking mechanism, although of the direct action type, was made in the substantial way that most fitments of the period were constructed. But, until the dramatic innovations of the 1870s, coaching stock remained a direct descendant of the stage coach building practices and even the eight-wheeled 'Long Charleys' introduced by the Great Western Railway in 1852 retained the rounded windows through which passengers had viewed the scenery of England for centuries. Many four- and six-wheeled vehicles continued to be built since, with a weight below 15 tons, only 30ft long and capable of carrying sixty passengers on moderately padded seats, such vehicles were too economical to be lightly discarded.

These middle years of the century thus remained a very mixed period when no two railways were alike, trains were made up of a great variety of different rolling stock and travelling on them was a mixture of excitement and tedium. On a long journey the absence of toilet, heating and refreshment facilities made the stops come as a welcome relief. Most lines had scheduled refreshment stops and places like Swindon, York and Preston became scenes of hectic activity as long distance trains allowed their passengers an average of 20 minutes to relieve themselves and try their luck in the queues in the refreshment rooms. Most of these had an unsavoury reputation and none more so than the establishment at Swindon which the Great Western Railway had leased out to private contractors. Within four years the company regretted their action and were taken to court when they tried to avoid the requirement to stop for 10 minutes. This millstone hung round the neck of the Great Western's train running department until 1895 when it cost the company £100,000 to buy themselves out of the arrangement.

As train speeds became more and more important the refreshment stops became more and more of a hindrance to competitive running. Stopping times were pared down in the interests of faster schedules or of recovering lost time and the subject provided the newspaper correspondence columns with a continuous source of complaining letters. One solution to the problem was the luncheon basket which made its appearance in 1871 and soon became a regular feature of railway travel. As the facility developed it became possible to obtain a very reasonable meal for a reasonable price. On the Great Western Railway route to the West luncheon and refreshment baskets were obtainable at Paddington, Bristol, Taunton, Exeter St Davids and Plymouth (Millbay and North Road) and offered a choice of a hot or cold meal for just 2s 6d. The latter would consist of cold meat or pie and salad, with cake and fruit and with claret available for an extra 1s 3d or beer for 1s (6d for a small bottle). Guards would despatch free the telegram ordering the baskets and first class passengers were also given the opportunity to hire a small folding table on payment of a further 6d.

The Great Northern railway pioneered the provision of foot warmers in 1852 in an attempt to alleviate one of the other great discomforts of railway travel. Initially the facility was for first class passengers only, but it was gradually extended until highly organised arrangements were in operation on most lines. The foot warmers were metal canisters filled with hot water and the Great Western Railway stocked up its supplying stations at the end of October each year and issued instructions covering both their use and the stations designated to change them — Bristol, Plymouth, Birmingham, Gloucester and Landore for fast trains, Swindon, Exeter, Oxford, Leamington and Shrewsbury additionally for stopping trains. Applying from the first day of November, the company then stipulated:

> At the Starting Station one warmer must be placed in each *First and Second Class* Compartment in All Through, and long Journey Trains, and others must be kept ready and supplied, if required by the passengers. *Third Class* passengers must be supplied with warmers when they ask for them.

Apparently not everyone benefited for a letter dated 1 January 1875 complained that, although the Great Northern and Midland were supplying them, 'there are no foot-warmers to be had on the South Western.' In the same newspaper and on the same day a Great Northern season ticket holder objected to the fact that he could not get a foot warmer 'without bribing a porter'.

For those with extra long journeys or a high regard for comfort there were many ways of easing the spartan nature of railway travel. The hip flask was a common accoutrement for gentlemen and a judicious nip from time to time would help to keep the cold away. Smoking might also add a little warmth to the atmosphere although this was officially discouraged until the Eastern Counties Railway heralded a change of attitude when it introduced a smoking saloon in 1846. Ladies used muffs to keep their hands warm and in winter a travelling rug was an essential part of the travel paraphernalia. A book to read was another essential, maybe one of the many railway guides which seemed as important to a railway traveller then as Michelin became to a later age. To make good the shortcomings of the pot lamps a travel candle would not only enable you to read your guide but also add a little warmth in the colder weather. In the warmer

Cover of the 1890 London, Tilbury and Southend timetable

months, windows could be opened to supplement the roof ventilators, the drop light window having been inherited from the coaching tradition and continuing as standard right up to recent years. Nor did railway travel escape the passion for novelty and invention, a complicated rubber gadget being discreetly advertised for those who 'needed relief before the advent of the next stopping point'.

Gas lighting came into use in the London area in 1862-3 but in a fairly primitive form and another twenty years were to pass before the replacement of oil as an illuminant became general policy on the Great Western Railway. The use of incandescent mantles from 1905 brought a great improvement in the quality of the lighting. The London, Brighton and South Coast Railway introduced its Pullman cars in 1881 and gave them electric lighting from accumulators carried in the guards van. Again there was a long interval between the first, experimental improvements and the adoption of a fully tested and efficient system as standard. Electric lighting became a standard provision for all new Great Western Railway stock from 1909, but years were to pass before gas lit vehicles disappeared altogether.

These slow but steady improvements in fitments were eclipsed in the last decades of the nineteenth century by fundamental changes in attitudes towards passengers and by accompanying transformations in coach design and train facilities. The pace setter in all this was the Midland Railway. Once it had its own London terminus that company seemed to set about establishing a reputation for getting business that it was to keep until the grouping of the railways in 1923. In the first instance it was by admitting third class passengers to all its trains from 1 April 1872 and three years later reducing the first class fares to the level of the abolished second class. Of this change in attitude to third class travel Sir James Allport, the Midland's general manager, was later to say: 'If there is one part of my public life on which I look back with more satisfaction than on anything else, it is with reference to the boon we conferred on third class passengers.' Not that the Midland's action was entirely altruistic for railway statistics were already beginning to show that the level of third class travel was increasing fast with the receipts per train mile much better than those of the other classes.

To celebrate another extension, this time the Settle and Carlisle line, the Midland made an arrangement with the Pullman Company for the latter to supply parlour cars and cars with combined drawing room, dining and sleeping facilities. The four- and six-wheel bogie vehicles put on the Scottish trains at the same period established standards which were to hold good for many years and forced the other companies, especially those operating over connecting or competing routes, to react. Some were quicker than others, the Great Eastern conveying third class passengers by all trains from 1 April 1872, the same day as the Midland, but the Great Western not taking the step until eighteen years later.

In addition to the effect of its early attitudes to less well off travellers, the Great Western Railway had the gauge problem to contend with. The company had introduced its first bogie carriage, 46ft long and with a clerestory roof, in 1874,

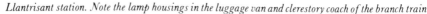

Llantrisant station. Note the lamp housings in the luggage van and clerestory coach of the branch train

The 'American Specials' boat trains ran between Liverpool and Euston to cater for the North American liner traffic. They used the new Riverside station in Liverpool from 1895

had abandoned iron spoked wheels and adopted the vacuum brake in the same period, but the construction of broad gauge vehicles did not cease until 1881 and even then the company had to build narrow-bodied stock on broad gauge frames with a view to conversion. Once the broad gauge had been swept away more rapid progress was possible and the company built its first corridor coach train — a set of five vehicles 50ft long and 8ft 8in wide — for the London to Birkenhead service, introduced steam heating in 1893 and added dining cars three years later. Elsewhere corridors leading to a lavatory compartment had been incorporated in a Great Northern Railway six-wheeled first class carriage design which had appeared in 1881 and by 1889 the Midland was providing this facility in its third class stock and maintaining its reputation as a pacemaker. Despite its rustic reputation, the Great Eastern was also an innovative company and had put on a dining saloon which served meals to the adjacent second and third class vehicles even before this facility appeared on the Scottish express services in 1893.

Sleeping cars as we know them, based on the single berth compartment rather than a travelling bed-sofa, derived from a North Eastern Railway design of 1895 although provision for sleeping on trains dates back to the earliest days. The bed carriage concept originated with the Grand Junction Railway and the London and Birmingham Railway and first appeared in 1838 as a combined mail and sleeping vehicle based upon a cushion supported between the seats and extra foot

43

A crowded platform at Lampeter. The photograph is inscribed Lampeter send off to a party of the 9th Welsh', probably during World War I

room in the boot part. A similar facility continued to be available for many years and the poles used to support the central cushion could be hired from train guards. The North British broke the tradition with a development in 1873 which provided a purpose-built sleeper vehicle for the East Coast route. In addition to two sleeping compartments and lavatories, there was a compartment for servants and another for luggage.

Many of these special facilities developed from the provisions made for the very ill or the very rich. Special vehicles were generally part of the same development as the family saloon which, in turn, had been part of the earliest round of variations from the standard accommodation pattern. The Great Western Railway experimented with a 'posting carriage' which, with its furnishings of tables and sofas, translated the family setting — so important at that period — into the train journey, just as the post chaise had sought to do in the road era.

The family saloon came further into its own as the holiday habit developed. When the better off family went to the seaside or spa resort in the late 1800s, it did so in style. Not for them the snatched weekend break or camping in the open air, but rather four to six weeks in a respectable seaside boarding house or the family's country home. The whole household moved, servants, luggage, children and pets, and nothing less than recreating a home away from home was acceptable. Changing trains would have been unthinkable — and nearly impossible — so a family saloon was hired at the originating point. It would be routed via suitable exchange points and there transferred from the rear of the train of one company to the onward service agreed in advance with the next one. The saloon layout usually provided a central luggage compartment with two further compartments on either side. One pair would be for the family elders and the children with their governess and the other for the domestic staff.

As the seaside habit spread to those of more modest incomes it still remained a major event. Weeks were spent in planning the arrangements, no one travelled light and the selection of accommodation on arrival was a careful and lengthy ritual. Once settled Mama would still preside over the domestic matters, visiting the shops each morning, arranging for the delivery of her purchases and then instructing the landlady as to the way they were to be prepared for the evening meal. The rise in real earnings at the end of the nineteenth century was accompanied by the establishment of holiday entitlements, and with the medical profession suddenly convinced that fresh air was not harmful as it had once supposed, railway trains to the coast at holiday times frequently ran in several portions. The better off who might not like this trend merely extended their travels to Europe and recreated the atmosphere they wanted in the resorts of Switzerland and the Riviera.

Another growth business for railways was commuter traffic. The trend began in London as early as 1838 when the London and Greenwich line opened and in 1840 when the cable-hauled trains of the London and Blackwall Railway first tried to abstract traffic from the river steamers. Both schemes, perhaps a little before their time, did well by allowing the use of their London terminus by other lines, but in the second half of the century the network of lines around London expanded rapidly and by the 1870s other large cities were beginning to develop commuter networks.

As a new century came into being the railway network of Great Britain had reached a total of 18,665 miles, annual passenger carryings exceeded 1,000 million and receipts were over £100m. Seventy years after the modest beginnings of the Liverpool and Manchester Railway the *Flying Scotsman* was running with full dining facilities and corridor access throughout. The 20-minute luncheon stop at York became a thing of the past and a new century ushered in a new railway era.

ATTITUDES AND INCIDENTS 5

Accepting that many of the letters to newspapers arise only from extreme incidents or feelings and that the everyday job well done rarely excites comment, nevertheless the correspondence columns of the nineteenth-century newspapers, the dramas conjured up by their reporters and the raillery of the contributors to *Punch* do provide a picture of railways of the period and of the view taken of them. The view is both fascinating and revealing and is not available to the same extent in the twentieth century, for writers seemed to have forsaken their railway grievances by the 1920s and turned instead to sanitation and plumbing.

The recent Milk Marketing Board exhortation to consume a pint of milk daily has its parallels back in the period when this interest in railways was so voluble. One of the many rhymes of the early years suggested the desirability of hanging a railway director daily:

> That those who the face of the country destroy
> And hurl o'er the best scenes of Nature alloy —
> Who Earth's brightest portions cut through at a dash —
> Who mix beauty and beastliness all in one hash . . .
> Base scum of the Earth, and sweet Nature's dissectors,
> Meet with no just reward — these same railway Directors!
> In this style I'd proceed, 'till I'd proved to the House
> That these railways, in fact, were a national chouse,
> And the best thing to do for poor Earth, to protect her,
> Would be — *to hang daily a Railway Director!*

Generally speaking the outpourings about railways in the early years were exceedingly long and of a pretty poor standard, but some contained a sufficient reflection of reality to be uncomfortable. Proclaiming that 'since railway accidents are inevitable . . . a salutary dread of them should be implanted in the minds of our rising generation', *Punch* gives four nursery rhymes in an 1852 issue. To be sung to the tune of 'Hush-a-by Baby', one reads:

> Rock away, passenger in the third class,
> When your train shunts a faster will pass;
> When your train's late your chances are small;
> Crushed will be carriages, engine and all.

Just how prophetic this was became clear in the following year when an unhappy accident on the Glasgow and South Western Railway had the dubious distinction of being the first to be reported on by the Board of Trade which involved fatalities in double figures. The location was Straffan and the date 5 October 1853. The time interval system of despatching trains was in operation and when a passenger train broke down and was not properly protected, a following goods train ran into the rear of the failed train killing fifteen people.

The dangers of travel, real and imagined, frequently occupied the writers in *Punch*. Nor were they slow in offering solutions either, including the somewhat unseemly suggestion that a van full of stokers should travel in the front of first class carriages 'since railways must have a glut of them as they are so liberal of stokers' lives'. Failing this another idea was to put a second or third class carriage behind each engine so that in the event of an accident 'only second or third class lives would be lost'.

In an effort to be more positive, *Punch* offered a 'New Grand National and Universal Steam Insurance, Railroad Accident and Partial Mutilation Provident Society', explaining that 'by the constitution of the society, the whole of the profits will be divided among such of the assured as can come to claim them.' The rates of insurance were set down as:

	£	s	d
First Class, leg	1	11	6
Second ditto ditto	1	7	9
First Class, arm	1	0	0
Second ditto ditto		14	3
First Class, bridge of nose (very common with cuts from glass)		8	9
Second ditto ditto (common with contusions from wooden frames)		6	4
First Class, teeth each			9
Whole set	1	1	0
Second ditto ditto			4¾
Whole set		12	2

and the address for enquiries given as 'The Branch Office, New Highgate Cemetery'.

Stokers were again given special mention in the *Punch* parody of this new business for the insurance companies. Their rates would be less if scalds were excluded and a liberal allowance was offered 'to such as the trains have passed over more than once'. Behind all this typical *Punch* treatment lay the very real fact that injuries to footplate crews were high and that travellers in the early open coaches were very much at risk.

A certain amount of adjustment had to be made by those who changed from travelling by coach to travelling by train. *Punch* took up the cudgels for a man fined 20s for going past his destination. The unfortunate passenger had fallen asleep and the magazine asked whether it was 'fare' to fine a man accustomed to taking his naps at 10mph and unable to adjust 'for the difference of travelling between a four-in-hand and a thirty horse power engine'. A writer in 1841 put it graphically when he complained, 'I missed Wolverton and Weedon while taking

Cheltenham in 1906. Not too much has changed although the water tank has gone, the lamps are electric and the Midland and South Western no longer offers a route to Southampton and Paris

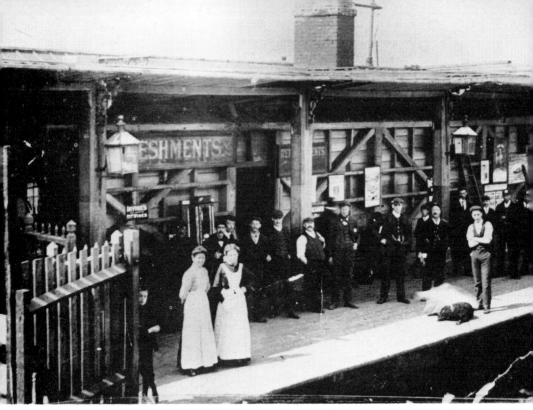

The first Tilbury (Riverside) station, complete with staff parade, advertisements, oil lamps and chocolate machine

a pinch of snuff, lost Rugby and Coventry before I had done sneezing, and I scarcely had time to say, "God Bless us," till I found we had reached Birmingham.' He proposed, for the benefit of travelling readers, to patent books suitable for rapid journeys and in which:

> only the actual spirit of the narration should be retained, rejecting all expletives, flourishes and ornamental figures of speech; to be terse and abrupt in style — use monosyllables always in preference to polysyllables — and to eschew all heroes and heroines whose names contain more than four letters....

Then, as now, more people complained than praised, but the complaints are a measure of the increasing use of the system and often cast light on contemporary attitudes and practices. A writer to *The Times* in 1848 accused the Great Western of trickery in withdrawing cheap return tickets. He wrote:

> Quite suddenly, and with only a few days notice, the most convenient trains are taken off, and the benefits derived from the return tickets are done away with also .... Such an act can scarcely be regarded in any other light than an open breach of faith .... All the unfortunate dupes — and I am one of the number — who have made their arrangements for living in the country, are now left in the lurch and to do the best they can ....

and in doing so revealed that the railways were even then influencing urban development patterns.

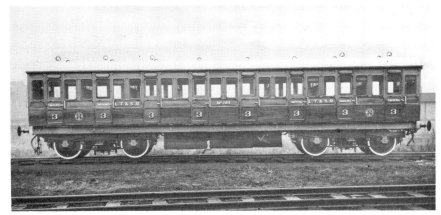

One of the 8-compartment, all third, bogie coaches introduced by the London, Tilbury and Southend in 1910

Complaints about the lack of punctuality were legion. The South Eastern Railway had a particularly unsavoury reputation in this respect. At a meeting chaired by Sir Charles Oakley at Cranbrook in 1881 it was alleged that the trains between Staplehurst and London lost an average of 25 minutes en route. Sir Edward Watkin promised Dover Town Council, a few years later, that an enquiry would be held into South Eastern Railway punctuality, but a cynical reporter attributed this primarily to the fact that Sir Edward himself, then chairman of the railway, had been delayed at Deal on 1 September 1895 'much to the amusement of his fellow travellers'.

Another four years on and *The Times* was devoting two and a half columns to the vexed subject of punctuality. It opened by avowing 'the marvel is, not that some trains are late, but that any train ever runs to time at all. Public opinion in England is in the long run practically irrestistible, and all the signs go to show that public opinion will before long insist on a higher standard of punctuality than is attained today.' In contrast, the piece ended with the conclusion that, despite their lack of punctuality, British trains were still 'the best in the world'. In between, it commented on most of the main railways; for example:

praising the Great Eastern and Great Northern companies and commenting, of King's Cross, 'Let those who have seen the helpless collapse of Continental management when a contretemps occurs say whether the country that invented railways cannot still give the world some lessons in the working of them.'

saying, about the Great Western, 'As long as the 3 o'clock express was first and second class only, it could just manage as a rule to keep time, but this summer its punctuality had been drowned beneath an inundation of third class passengers.'

and warning, in connection with the London and North Western Railway, 'Dark whispers are heard that this summer chaos has more than once invaded the cosmos of Euston.'

Complaints about railway employees appeared regularly in the newspapers. No doubt some were justified for the workforce was large — 100,000 halfway through the century — and the tradition of the railway family in which succeeding generations served the same company was still to come. In the early years the growing railways needed increasing numbers of staff and many came from agriculture, labouring and factories in search of better pay and a more stable way of life. Not all were suitable. 'One Concerned' complained about the treatment accorded to his wife and the two children with her when she changed at Castleford. With one of the infants barely a month old, the weather wet and miserable and the journey from Manchester to Hull seeming interminable, the lady complained when shown to an open carriage. She continued to remonstrate with the guard whose patience eventually evaporated and led him to remark, 'Come on, if you're coming' as he pushed the reluctant brood into the offending vehicle. Perhaps he was justified, if only to avoid more letters about punctuality, but in his letter the aggrieved husband thundered, 'Cannot such tyranny be stopped? Are the weak and unprotected of our community to be left at the mercy of these iron monopolists?'

Another writer complained about the service between the Eastern Counties Railway station at Peterborough and the one on the Great Northern, a mile and a half away:

> Yet let anyone make trial — on a Saturday at any rate — and he will find himself at the close of the experiment in a state of mind very far from right.... A long period is consumed in the collection of fourpenny fares, an operation conducted with an aristocratic deliberation and negligence perfectly charming. When you rush at the Great Northern train, which you are allowed to see slowly moving away, you are of course stopped on the ground of 'no ticket'. It is a trying moment, one in which you remember Job and forget your decalogue .... With the officials on the Eastern Counties Railway I have no particular fault to find; they are apathetic, of course, and occasionally mendacious, but by no means uncivil.

London and South Western Railway 2-4-0 Tartar *built in 1870 with 6ft 6in driving wheels and rudimentary cab*

Tipping got fairly regular exposure in the correspondence columns. In 1871 a writer complained that he could not get anything done without giving a sixpenny tip. Without this his luggage 'was always left to last'. The rate for ticket inspectors was higher, for the same complainant was apparently 'not allowed to see a lady to her carriage without giving a shilling to the ticket inspector'. He then turned his attention to Waterloo where the problem arose when changing between South Eastern and South Western trains and, we are informed, 'the former porters will take luggage to the limit of their premises, but then you have to pay an outside porter to take it any further.'

The distinctions between the different classes of travel and the times of heavy traffic movements both prompted a fair share of the letters about railways. In August 1858 a man was upset because he had paid the first class fare only to find that all the accommodation on his train was reserved for Lord Carrington's party. Waiting for a later train brought no improvement in the availability of seats so he complained to the railway and the press. For the latter one J.S.S. Talbot of the 'Pimlico Terminus' explained, 'There was a lot of second and third class that day as it was the occasion of the charity children to the Palace.'

When a man objected to passengers with second class tickets travelling in a first class carriage he was told that there was 'nowhere else for them'. He then had to suffer for his action:

> For the next half hour we had the felicity of listening to abuse of first class passenger carriages and other disagreeable conversation from our fellow travellers, who, knowing they had been objected to, naturally took that mode of revenge.

Another first class ticket holder complained to a porter that the first class carriage was overcrowded with people 'of the humblest class'. 'Come out of it yourself, then,' was the only suggestion he got for his trouble.

Other correspondents wrote about cancelled trains, fares anomalies, journeys which would have been faster by cab and even having to show one's ticket too often — six times between Charing Cross and Maidstone. The late issue of timetables was alleged to be deliberate 'so that companies can play a cat-and-mouse game, trying to overreach each other'. Physical incidents were also described, including one headed 'Sixty Miles on a Broken Spring' and describing how passengers were jolted all the way to Herne Hill after a spring broke while passing through Faversham. Revealingly, the describer of the incident added that 'attempts to pull the communication cord were futile as it was quite loose'.

The use of the railway system for the purposes of suicide and disposing of unwanted babies — usually in a brown paper parcel on the luggage rack, under the seat or left in a waiting room — was soon in vogue, but other incidents are more revealing of the times. A porter at the Lancaster and Carlisle Railway's Castle station, on a winter's day in 1847, found a child in one of the carriages, neatly tucked in a basket and labelled 'To Be Called For'. The child was taken to the workhouse but in the evening the father called at the station and the circumstances surrounding this unusual consignment were revealed. According to the reporter of the incident, 'It seems that he [the father] is a coachmaker on tramp, and hearing, while at Kendal, of the probability of meeting with work at

Lancaster, despatched [the child] thither per railway, while he performed the journey on foot.'

Vandalism was a problem in the last century, as it is today, and in adults it was frequently combined with drunkenness. In 1847 there was a serious case in which a section of rail was removed from the line shortly before a Taff Vale Railway passenger train was due. The train locomotive and three carriages were derailed and serious injuries were only avoided because, in a typical Welsh 'valleys' line situation, the derailed vehicles fell towards the hillside instead of towards the river. For this malicious act one William Scott was sentenced at the Quarter Sessions at Cardiff on 8 January 1848 to seven years deportation.

Bullets were fired at trains and stones thrown at them — and in at least one case reported the two boys involved in the latter 'were later apprehended by the police and handed over to their parents to be birched'. In other cases ladies were assaulted and luggage stolen and at Blackburn a ruffian who delighted in insulting ladies as trains entered a tunnel was caught by a detective dressed in female clothing. In another case the Eastern Counties Railway was having trouble in 1853 with the loss of luggage from vans forwarded from its Shoreditch depot to various stations throughout the system. In an effort to detect the thieves a man was concealed in one of the vans for several nights. In due course this manoeuvre paid off and the hidden policeman apprehended a young man who had scrambled into the van intent upon thowing out suitable items for his accomplices to catch. The hunt for the latter continued and Inspector Goring and another policeman came across three men late one night near Temple Mills. They were talking and looking for packages along the lineside and fled as soon as they spotted the representatives of the law. The one chased by the inspector dived into the River Lea in an attempt to escape, but the policeman dived in after him and the two struggled in the water. The thief did manage to break free and reach the bank but only to fall back in the water and disappear from view, 'presumed drowned' as the newspaper put it.

Luggage vans featured in one of the many reports of runaway trains. In this case the report comes from the *Halifax Guardian* of 27 April 1848. Two Manchester and Huddersfield Railway porters at Huddersfield station apparently forgot to apply the handbrakes on two luggage vans standing in the station for unloading. Since the line was on a gradient the vehicles, not surprisingly, set off down the incline and were soon speeding away at 20mph towards the junctions at Bradley. With great presence of mind Mr Hirst, the station master, found himself an engine, climbed aboard with the driver, stoker and the station's head porter and 'set off at full speed after the runaways'. It took them three miles of chasing and careful engine handling to get the head porter into a position where he could hook the errant vans to the locomotive from a highly precarious position on the latter's buffer beam.

Some incidents did not end so well. Two breakaway collisions occurred within two years of one another and involved the deaths of twenty-five passengers. On 23 August 1858 at Round Oak on the Oxford, Worcester and Wolverhampton line part of a heavily loaded passenger train broke away on a gradient and ran back into a following train, and then on 4 September 1860 on the Lancashire and Yorkshire Railway an excursion train was involved in a similar accident.

Two other incidents will suffice to demonstrate the range of experiences offered by rail travel in the last century. In one an artist, Mr Ellis, was travelling on the London and North Western Railway in 1874 and encountered two fellow travellers who were to turn his journey into a nightmare. They were Thomas Holmes and his father, both the worse for the drink Thomas had been buying for the best part of a week since the burial of his wife. Hardly had the train left Runcorn than the younger Holmes drew a knife and attempted to cut the throat of the unfortunate Mr Ellis. The latter's offer of his purse was treated with drunken scorn and the purse, with £8 inside, pitched through the open window. Ellis, now bleeding from the face and neck, tried to restrain his attacker and Holmes senior sobered up enough to join in. But the grief-crazed Thomas Holmes was beyond restraint or reason. He slipped from the artist's clutches, bit off the luckless man's right thumb in the process and then clambered out of the carriage window. There he remained, as if exhausted by his frenzy, until the train stopped and he fell unconscious to the track and an eventual journey to the cells.

A simpler, happier event was reported from the west bank of the Severn:

. . . we felt the train suddenly stop, and looking out to the front we saw, to our astonishment, the driver jump off the engine, vault the fence and proceed to fill his hat with the mushrooms. In a moment the guard was over the fence following his example which, as may be supposed, was infectious, for in less than half a minute every door was thrown open and the field covered with passengers every one of whom brought back a pretty good hatful.

Fortunately some events turned out less serious and almost had a funny side. One such is revealed in an 1860 report of what happened at 5 o'clock on an April morning at Penzance when a half awake cleaner had moved an engine without either completely closing the regulator or fully applying the brake afterwards:

On his return the engine was gone . . . the fire had caught quickly, steam rose, and away went the riderless puffer over the wooden viaduct at Chyandour, smashing through the gates at Marazion station, slowly up the incline, 60 miles an hour down steep gradients, over many unoccupied crossings, through numerous pairs of stout gates, by St Ives Road and Hayle, Gwinear Road and Camborne, until its breath was nearly gone. The first of a pair of gates near Pool it opened, the second it tore up and bore along the line on its cow-catcher, until at Carn Brea someone saw it coming at an abated speed, with the gate in front, jumped on it, and thus secured the truant — most fortunately not the slightest harm having occurred except to the gates aforesaid during its unrestrained run of 16 or 17 miles.

THE GREAT YEARS

6

By 1900 the main line railway system in Great Britain had largely stabilised. The only major developments of this period were the Great Central Railway London extension and improvements like those on the Great Western Railway which produced the direct route to South Wales via Badminton, the cut-off route to the West via Westbury and the new Bristol to Birmingham main line via Honeybourne. The branch lines continued to increase and the light railway legislation of 1896 produced some fascinating routes in rural areas. From 18,665 miles in 1900 the route mileage operated by the principal railways rose to 19,979 miles by 1910, 20,326 by 1920 and 20,445 by 1930. But much of the new light railway mileage was in the form of electric tramways and the branch line and rural developments were to prove vulnerable to economies necessitated by the 1914-18 war, the General Strike of 1926 and the increasing impact of motor bus competition. By 1940 a contraction was apparent and by 1960 the system was back to its size at the turn of the century.

In the main the great railways which had emerged from the years of construction and amalgamation turned from their expansionist policies of the nineteenth century to a search for higher standards of speed, comfort and operational efficiency. In the process the passengers benefited greatly, the corridor express with dining facilities became the norm for the prestige routes, all-steel coaches appeared, electric lighting and cooking were no longer novelties and a high proportion of vehicles had toilet facilities. The era of the spartan, short wheelbase box was over, although many old vehicles lingered on to serve those branch lines which did not warrant an allocation of the railcars which began to appear. In at least one case old gas lit vehicles had to be kept in service because the operation of mixed trains on a remote West Country branch meant speeds insufficient to generate electric lighting.

The new Great Central Railway kept its rivals on their toes. It proclaimed 'Rapid Travel in Luxury' as its theme, adding on the front of its timetables 'Each Express is Vestibuled and has a Buffet Car Attached for First and Third Class Passengers'. In its 'Notices for July 1903' the Great Central Railway detailed three new expresses and four new through-carriage facilities on the main line bringing the total of through carriage linkings up to 256. There were also improved services between London and Stratford-upon-Avon, across country via Banbury and Newbury, between Liverpool and Hull, to and from the Great Eastern via Lincoln, from Lincolnshire to London and to Warrington, North Wales and the Cheshire Lines Committee stations. Grimsby for Esbjerg was

A typical country station, in this case Ketton

Prestigious stations required appropriate architecture: the striking frontage of Bristol Temple Meads station

stressed as the 'Quick Route' to Denmark and the Hotel Great Central as the 'Favourite Rendezvous for Travellers from the North'.

Before the twentieth century was three years old the Mersey Railway had been electrified, on 3 May 1903, electric trains appearing on the Lancashire and Yorkshire line between Liverpool and Southport in the following year and on the Inner Circle in 1905. The London and South Western introduced automatic signalling on the Andover to Grateley section in 1902 and four years later the Great Western Railway started to run trains with audible cab signalling, first on the double track Henley branch, then on the single line to Fairford and, from

East Ham station around 1925, and only one car in view

1908, on the first section of main line. Full ATC introduction was to wait for some time, like the development of the ideal railbus, but the era of innovation and change had started to show its first dividends.

As the major cities expanded electric tramways started to take passengers away from the inner suburban trains and the railways responded in a variety of different ways. Some, like the Glasgow and South Western, bowed to the inevitable, others decided to fight. What is now the huge network of electrified lines on the Southern Region began with the London, Brighton and South Coast's electrification of the route from Victoria to London Bridge via the South London line from 1 December 1909 with the Battersea Park to Crystal Palace (Low Level) section following two years later. In 1912 the Crystal Palace to Selhurst and the Peckham Rye to West Norwood lines were added, all on the overhead system which later gave way to third rail. At this period the London, Brighton and South Coast was advertising *The Southern Belle* as consisting of '7 luxuriously appointed Pullman Cars (4 Parlour, 1 Buffet and Smoking, and 2 Smoking Cars) exquisitely upholstered, lighted by electricity, comfortably warmed and ventilated, and fitted with all the latest improvements'. Taking exactly an hour from Victoria to Brighton the two weekday down services left Victoria at 11am and 3.10pm and the up services set off from Brighton at 12.20pm and 5.45pm. There were 'Pullman Drawing Room Cars' to both Brighton and Eastbourne, a wealth of services to the Continent and the joint London and North Western Railway and London, Brighton and South Coast *Sunny South Special* pulling out of Liverpool Lime Street at 11am as the northbound working left Hastings at the same time.

The railway search for speed had started well before the turn of the century, on the East and West Coast routes to Scotland following the completion of the Forth Bridge in 1890, and between the Great Western and London and South Western companies for the Ocean Liner traffic from Plymouth. The latter produced the

Barking station looking east about 1906

great run of *City of Truro* on the Great Western Railway Ocean Mail run in 1904 when a speed of 102.3mph was reached on the descent of Whiteball summit, news considered too dramatic to be released at the time for fear of alarming the travellers of the day. It also led to the calamitous accident in 1906 when London and South Western Railway engine No 421, with a train of five coaches and the passengers off the American liner *New York*, took the reverse curves at Salisbury too fast and twenty-eight people lost their lives.

The 1914-18 war hit the nation and its railways hard. It also showed clearly the need for their restructuring and this became a fact by virtue of the Railways Act, 1921, implemented in the grouping of 1923. For several years the energies of the new 'Big Four' were consumed in getting themselves organised, with the Southern becoming absorbed in its electrification programme from the mid-1920s, the Great Western Railway sorting out its new docks and coal empire in South Wales and the London, Midland and Scottish Railway trying to reconcile old differences between the haughty 'Premier Line', the thrusting Midland and the parochial interests of the other constituents.

On the London and North Eastern Railway the Gresley Pacifics appeared in 1924 and, following the valve gear design modifications suggested by the comparison trials with the Great Western Railway *Castle* class, the London and North Eastern Railway's new big engines were ready to lift the railway community out of the dismal years of post war reconstruction and national economic depression. The world's longest non-stop run was achieved by the company from 1 May 1928 when the 4-6-2s started to work between King's Cross and Edinburgh using corridor tenders to allow a change of footplate crew without stopping. By 1932 the Great Western Railway's 'Cheltenham Flyer' was averaging 71.3mph over the Swindon to Paddington leg of its journey, but speeds

Southern Railway N15 4-6-0 No 788 at the head of a good sized train

1937 London, Midland and Scottish Coronation Class 4-6-2 6229 Duchess of Hamilton, *streamlined even down to the headlamps*

of over 100mph in trial runs down Stoke Bank south of Grantham in 1934-5 suggested that the London and North Eastern Railway was aiming for something even more dramatic.

The secret was closely guarded but everyone associated with railways knew there was something in the wind and then, on 27 September 1935, it happened. Less than a month after the Great Western Railway celebrated its centenary a silver-grey train headed by a streamlined *Silver Link* carrying members of the Press twice touched 112mph and exceeded the magic 100mph for over 25 miles. The public service which followed was a great success. Small boys were taken to see the new streamliners, their devotees applauded the new look in interior design, engineers discussed the merits of articulating the coaches and the public took the service to its heart and cheerfully paid the fare supplements. This commercial success for the 'Silver Jubilee' service linking Kings Cross and Darlington non-stop had led, within two years, to the 'Coronation' service to Edinburgh and to the London, Midland and Scottish 'Coronation Scot' to Glasgow. The former involved a 71.9mph booking for the 188.2 miles between Kings Cross and York to snatch the 'Cheltenham Flyer's' mantle and the latter clocked up a new record of 114mph on the trial run. Then even the latter was made to look modest by the consequences of a note from Sir Nigel Gresley during the 1938 brake tests. He 'proposed to run the train to Barkston and back in order that a fast run down the bank from Stoke Tunnel may be recorded' — the outcome was a 126mph world steam record for *Mallard* which has never been bettered.

These were the great days on Britain's railways. Not always glamorous and efficient as some descriptions imply, but always interesting. Extremely busy too, with the hefty editions of Bradshaw running to over a thousand pages and detailing services as different as the $98\frac{1}{4}$ mile cross country adventure over the

4033 is putting everything into getting hold of the nine-coach train working of the 11.45am Bristol to Paddington

border from Carlisle to Edinburgh via Hawick and Galashiels, and those despatched staccato from stations like London Bridge and Victoria. There was hardly a period on the main lines when something was not going on. At King's Cross, for example, the only lull was between the departure of the 1.05am Edinburgh sleeper, closely followed by the 1.10am to Leeds, and the resumpton of activity at 4.45am when the early morning service to York departed. First stop Peterborough, this train then did a variety of jobs including calling at Essendine long before the two branch trains out to Stamford and Bourne started work. Not that they wouldn't have been worth waiting for as the Bourne branch train must have set a record for gleaming brasswork, and alighting at the charming GNR station at Stamford, set by the side of the river and influenced by the involvement of the Marquis of Exeter, was a real railway experience. In later years the signalman at the latter point had sufficient time to try his luck with the fish in the river without actually leaving his box, but that was certainly not the atmosphere back on the 4.45 when it called at the local stations south of Doncaster to pick up the commuters for that busy railway town.

The layout at King's Cross has been simplified since the London and North Eastern Railway days when it was no easy station to work. Up local trains were no problem if continuing on to Moorgate, but those terminating at the suburban station had to cross all lines serving the main station, locking up all train movements while they did so. The suburban trains from Moorgate emerged on the down side, but the platform was on a gradient and once the signalman had set the road, the N2 tank heading for New Barnet or Hertford might still spend

A typical small town station, in this case Stamford on the London, Midland and Scottish route from Peterborough to Leicester

several minutes of slipping, trying to get hold of its train but holding up other services waiting to pass through the tunnel bottleneck while it did so. Once on the move the N2 could prove quite sprightly and when two left Finsbury Park together the passengers herded in their respective Quad-Art sets could relieve the tedium of their commuter journeys by watching their fellow travellers jolt along with them, only inches away. Both would look with envy at those in the 'Garden Cities and Cambridge Buffet Express' trains whose $1\frac{1}{4}$-hour journey would be made in bogie stock and disdain any station south of Welwyn Garden City.

Euston station in the last days of the London, Midland and Scottish

A nice time to travel was by one of the morning trains, perhaps the 10 o'clock 'Flying Scotsman' or the 11 o'clock 'Scarborough Flyer'. In those pre-war days, when earnings were modest but you seemed to get value for what you spent, the Table d'Hote luncheon was only 3s 6d for the full five courses, or 2s 6d if you took only the main course fish or joint and the sweet or cheese. The half-crown price would thus command roast shoulder of mutton, onion sauce, brussel sprouts and jacket or mashed potatoes with gooseberry pudding or perhaps meringue chantilly to follow. Attractive tableware, good cutlery, flowers for decoration and spotless white table linen were all part of the experience.

Afternoon tea was another pleasant on-train ritual and dinner on 'The

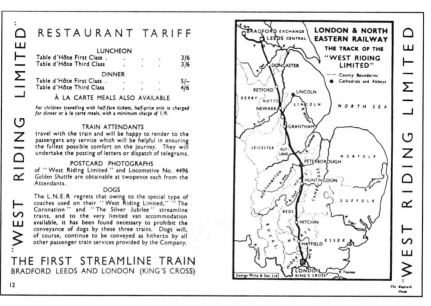

Pages from the London and North Eastern Railway publicity booklet of the 'West Riding Limited'

Yorkshire Pullman' or the 5.30pm 'Silver Jubilee' was an event of some distinction. Somehow the Pullman seemed particularly stately and looking in through those high windows at the shaded lamps and ornate surroundings might create as much envy on the part of the passenger for Nottingham or Boston as he had excited in the commuter bound for Cuffley or High Barnet. It was not just the comfort, for lesser trains with an Atlantic or a V2 up front — or perhaps a grimy K3 dragged off a coal train to stand in for a locomotive that had 'fallen down' — envied the A3 or A4 Pacific allocated and the right of prestige trains to the down main line and a good chance of clear signals.

For the traveller to an intermediate station on the main line the journey might be one of mixed fortunes. At one period a combined Peterborough and Cambridge train left King's Cross around 6pm and was double headed as far as Hitchin where the train split into its two portions. If things went well the local train could make some progress on the slow line while the West Riding and Hull services thundered past and the first of the evening sleepers steamed majestically by on the main line. But in the freezing winter fogs of those days before the Clean

Passengers in long coats, a bookstall, produce on a barrow and 5667 arriving at Sheffield in the 1930s

Air Act the journey could become a nightmare. As often as not there would be a late start waiting for an engine off an incoming service or for a chance to make the complicated manoeuvre to get from the shed, and then another wait at Hadley Wood which had not then been given an extra pair of running lines to Potters Bar. For the passengers living at Hatfield or taking the branch trains from there to St Albans, Dunstable or Hertford the sight of the familiar staggered platforms and grimy locomotive depot was a welcome one, but others still had to face the bottleneck at Welwyn where the high viaduct took the main line over the tiny Rim Ram river.

Those bound for the Peterborough line now began to look forward to the arrival at Hitchin. The wait there would be of several minutes while the Peterborough engine drew forward to let the train engine depart with the Cambridge portion and then set back onto its own. The practised traveller could use these to grab a quick drink in the refreshment room, taken standing as near as possible to the warmth of roaring fire. If his luck was out, the train might be ready to go forward before the queue had been dealt with and he would have to hurry back to his seat with nothing to fortify him for the second half of the journey. On such nights the lights usually grew steadily dimmer because the dynamo belt was slipping, the heat finally disappeared as it leaked away through perished steam pipes, the lavatory was out of order and the water can provided empty and there were waits to get onto the main line at Arlesey, Sandy and Huntingdon. The connection our traveller had wanted at Sandy would be late because the single-line staff had been dropped in the river during the exchange outside Bedford, or the connecting train at Huntingdon might be seen leaving the East station as he drew into the North, and if he changed at Holme for Ramsey it might be to find that the last train had left the former at 10.15am!

In these years in the first half of the century the great majority of those who travelled did so by train. There were still some remote communities where there was no railway and no one expected to go far anyway, but most families would make some use of the railway network even if it was only to travel to war or go with the Sunday School or works outing to Barry or Leigh-on-Sea. In any event there were no real alternatives until the 'thirties and even then the private car was making only a limited impact and the bus companies competed primarily for local travel, party business and the weekend holiday traffic.

The holiday periods demonstrated better than any the importance of the railway network. Trains ran in several portions and were supplemented by dozens of reliefs and still passengers had to stand. Christmas was one of the occasions when it never seemed to matter, the queue for the booking office or passimeter was accepted patiently, the late running and the impossible crush in the refreshment room were predictable and when the train did arrive the station inspector might have to get some of the doors closed by a hefty kick before giving the guard a green light, leaving those in the packed corridors to settle themselves down as best they could. Clutching luggage of every shape and size and settling the children on the nearest friendly knee, everyone seemed to accept these conditions as part of the traditional pilgrimages of Christmas and subordinated the discomfort to the anticipation of the festive season. For every family met at a main line station with a car, another had to complete its final journey by bus or arrive at a country station and tramp the last few miles over snow covered fields.

Life was much the same during the summer holiday period as trains left Waterloo and Paddington to drop portions or fill branch trains waiting at a dozen junctions along the route. Staff at the resorts wrestled to cope with

Veteran 0-6-0 7415 at Perth on a Dundee to Stirling train

luggage, cloakroom deposits, requests for advice on accommodation and a hundred and one other things. The resorts had been growing fast since the 1870s and by the twentieth century had tended to develop their own hinterlands. The south coast drew Londoners like a magnet and the resorts on either side of the Thames catered for those who wanted only a day trip or a short journey. Going to the Isle of Wight was a sort of small adventure, anticipated all the way down to Portsmouth Harbour and first realised as you walked across the gangplank of the paddle steamer which was to carry you across to the island. On the way a glimpse of a great liner, perhaps with one of those stirring names like *Berengaria,* would reveal an even more exotic world, but the little trains of the Southern Isle of Wight system, headed by a Stroudley 0-6-0T or an Adams 0-4-4T, had a presence all of their own and drove any such thoughts out of mind.

Blackpool, Southport, Morecambe and the Wirral served Lancashire and Scarborough or Whitby entertained Yorkshire. From Sheffield or the East Midlands you went to 'Skeggy' or Cleethorpes — as the Manchester, Sheffield and Lincolnshire Railway had intended you should — and from the West Midlands you went to Weston-super-Mare or Yarmouth depending on which side of Birmingham you lived. By this time Weston had put off the attitude that had confined its early railway facilities to a short, horse-worked line and welcomed the Midlanders to its excursion station or the fine station on the loop

A Manchester Central to Derby stopping train pulls into Millers Dale Station. Although this was a large station built primarily for the extensive limestone quarries nearby, it was also a very popular venue for ramblers to the Peak District

Upminster station in 1905 and platelayers stand back as No 63 rushes through with a Down Southend service

Down express double headed on the London and South Western main line to Portsmouth

Chester station in the 1930s. Barrow loads of churns and hampers are ready for loading on the arriving train

line. The golden sands of Yarmouth offered much needed relaxation after a long journey from Manchester, Leicester or Birmingham, something which could be a painful and wearying experience when trains got out of course on the long single line sections of the Midland and Great Northern route. What should have been a five-hour journey for the midnight departure from Manchester (Victoria) to Yarmouth might turn into double that time as the train tangled with the workings from the north via Essendine and Bourne, the other expresses via Castle Bytham and the King's Cross to Cromer through coaches. No wonder the stopping trains were allowed 80 minutes for the $37\frac{1}{2}$ miles from Peterborough to South Lynn, 164 minutes for the $52\frac{1}{4}$ miles from Saxby to South Lynn and another 179 minutes for the $73\frac{1}{4}$ miles on to Yarmouth.

In addition to this holiday business the railways continued to put considerable effort into securing excursion and party traffic. The former offered a range of venues, from the conventional day at the sea to visits to special events, sights and spectacles and the latter would arrange almost anything if twelve or more people could be found to see or do it. Excursions had been a feature of railway life from the 1850s onwards; a typical Great Western Railway excursion of 1858 from Salisbury for a 'Grand Floral Fete' at Bath attracted 263 passengers, but on an Easter Monday excursion to Weymouth only forty-four people travelled and the excursion diary reads:

> . . . very rainy, blowing a hurricane all day; the *Cygnus* steam packet from the [Channel] islands endeavoured to enter the Harbour five times before she could effect it — the S.W. packet refused to leave Weymouth.

Crowds at Leyburn on the London and North Eastern Railway (NE) awaiting the return of their excursion train after an outing to view the total eclipse of the sun in June 1927

Typical of the early part of this century was a Great Western 'Express Day Excursion Train' to the Military International Exhibition of 1901 when, for a payment of seven shillings, you could rise early enough to leave Cardiff at 5.10am and spend the journey deciding whether you wanted to see the 'Grand Military Spectacle — China and the Relief of the Legations', go to a Tonic Sol-Fa Festival at the Crystal Palace or take one of the New Palace Steamers from Old Swan Pier and go to Tilbury, Margate or Ramsgate — provided it would get you back to Paddington in time for a 12.50am return on Sunday morning. This outlook existed between 1898 when the Anti-Sunday Travelling Union had boasted 20,000 members and 1913 when restrictive attitudes towards travel on the Sabbath had been shouted down at a London and North Western Railway meeting. This 12.50am departure was carefully calculated to preserve the concept of a day (only) excursion without upsetting anyone's principles.

As the century progressed railway canvassers exhibited more and more imagination in their efforts to secure this optional business. As the buses offered cheaper fares for the straightforward journeys, the railways used their capacity to work with entertainment groups, caterers and others to provide more and more enticing outings. Steamers featured in many of these, from an educational trip for school parties when the historic significance of Runnymede had to compete with the excellent tea provided on the Salters vessels, to a journey all the way to Scotland and a sail on Loch Lomond or down the Clyde. In the Great Western's holiday country you could take the train from Exeter to Starcross, cross by steam launch to Exmouth and return to Exeter via the Southern route for 1s 6d. If 4s was not too much you could, instead, take the train to Totnes, enjoy the winding beauty of the River Dart and then travel back by train from Kingswear. Almost anything he might want was available to the party outing organiser. Theatre tickets were no trouble, meals could be fixed *en route* and there was a free ticket for the club secretary who put in so many unpaid hours in getting members to agree upon where they wanted to go.

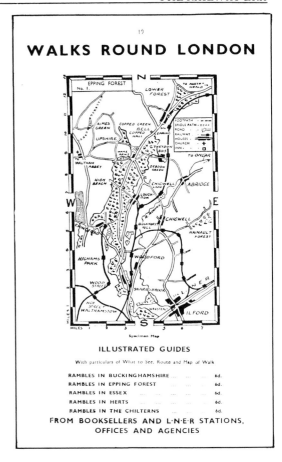

Some data from a London and North Eastern Railway pamphlet aimed at hikers and ramblers

The beauty of the party traffic business was that it could be accommodated on existing services and the same applied to encouraging travel by special interest groups. So the main line railways set out to woo hikers, ramblers, anglers, cyclists and the like. Special fares were offered for day, half-day or weekend outings and modestly priced guides were often made available describing routes, and what to see. For 6d the London and North Eastern Railway would supply a copy of *Rambles in Buckinghamshire* or, if you preferred, a similar booklet for Epping Forest, Essex, Hertfordshire or the Chilterns, and trips could be made from Marylebone to Chorley Wood and Chenies for 2s 6d or from the industrial Lea Valley to Maldon East on the Blackwater estuary for 4s 9d.

Away from the glamour of the express world and the excitement of a holiday or outing, hundreds of other lines served the needs of the local community. Some were substantial routes, once even proud main lines of some pre-grouping or pre-amalgamation company, others were mainly used by commuters and some were just meandering rail byways. Lines like that from Hellifield to Lancaster and Carnforth had a multiple role. It carried an all-stations service to meet local needs, but this also had to connect with more important lines at either end and keep out of the way of the through services, in this case the Isle of Man and Belfast Boat Expresses. Near the heartland of industrial Lancashire and Yorkshire

8

FOR A LONGER HOLIDAY
ASK FOR A
. TOURIST TICKET
issued 1st MAY to 31st OCTOBER
to
HEALTH AND HOLIDAY RESORTS
from
PRINCIPAL STATIONS

3rd Class   1st Class
15/-   **MINIMUM FARES**   22/6

The Tickets are available for 3 calendar months, and break of journey is permitted at intermediate
stations en route

INTERAVAILABILITY OF TICKETS
L M S, L N E & G.W. RAILWAYS
Passengers holding these tickets covering places served by the lines of all three of the L M S, L·N·E·R &
G.W. Companies, or of any two of them (including Joint Lines owned by any two of these Companies), are allowed
to travel on the RETURN journey between such places by any of the recognised routes of these Companies. Break
of journey is allowed to holders of the above-mentioned tickets at intermediate stations on the alternative route
Apply L·N·E·R Stations and Agencies for particulars

WEEKLY HOLIDAY SEASON TICKETS
1st APRIL to 31st OCTOBER
When spending your holidays in
SCOTLAND, NORTH EAST ENGLAND,
LINCOLNSHIRE OR EAST ANGLIA
Take a Weekly Season Ticket for Sightseeing Travel in Holiday Districts
FULL PARTICULARS CAN BE OBTAINED AT PRINCIPAL STATIONS

CIRCULAR TOUR TICKETS
If you desire a circular trip by rail; or rail, road and or steamer, to visit a number of
places in the British Isles over an extended period of three months ask for a Circular Tour
ticket. These are issued at about 1¼d. per mile third class point to point, and first class
travel is given approximately 50 per cent. higher fares

BARGAIN TRAVEL TICKETS
ON SUNDAYS
Between
ANY TWO STATIONS in ENGLAND and WALES
on
G.W.R., L M S and L·N·E·R
(including Joint Lines)
RETURN FARES
THIRD CLASS—APPROXIMATELY SINGLE FARE
FIRST CLASS—50 PER CENT ABOVE THIRD CLASS
Minimum Fares, Third Class 2/6 : First Class 3/9
AVAILABLE BY ANY TRAIN ON DAY OF ISSUE ONLY :
OUTWARD—By any train leaving at or after 12.0 midnight on Saturday Sunday
RETURN —By any train leaving up to midnight on Sunday
INTERAVAILABILITY :
Passengers holding these tickets, covering places served by the lines of all three of the G.W., L M S and
L·N·E·R Companies, or of any two of them (including Joint Lines owned by any two of these Companies), are
allowed to travel on the RETURN journey between such places by any of the recognised routes of these Companies

P4/109 22   Printed at the L.N.E.R Company's Printing Works, Stratford Market   S.7474.38   20,000

*A few of the many examples of
special fares and tickets*

hundreds of trains criss-crossed the landscape serving the mill and factory workers, the shoppers and the visitors; the steel and shipbuilding industries of the North East had a train service related to their shift work pattern, other trains pottered through the Fens or struggled through the mountains of North Wales and away to the north in Scotland the lonely line from Inverness to Wick could occupy the traveller from 10.25am to 4.19pm unless he waited until 4.10pm to save three hours by travelling on 'The John o'Groat'. Unfortunately by the time this arrived at Wick the 13½-mile light railway to Lybster had closed for the day and the weary passenger was stranded. Unless, that is, he had the wisdom to travel on a Saturday when railways catered for such long distance passengers in trains whose primary function was to serve the late reveller, in this case the 10.45pm from Wick calling at Thrumster, Ubster, Mid Clyth and Occumster and at the line's three halts if required.

On market days many of the branch services would be packed tight with country folk going to sell or buy, or perhaps just to find a little relief from the long hours and arduous nature of pre-war farming. They would have walked to the station from local cottages, been brought in by the village bus, cycled or made the journey in style by pony and trap. The ticket clerk would have been kept busy in the short hectic period before the train was due, but he could remove the card

Oban station overlooked by its town

A Perth-Edinburgh train in the beautiful scenery around Glenfarg

from its tube, date it without catching his thumb painfully in the press and have the change calculated and ready in no time unless the rhythm was disturbed by the complication of a cycle storage ticket, one for a pram or dog, or someone wanted to make a travel enquiry or present a warrant.

There would ·be a stir among the crowd on the platform as the knowing recognised the single bell of the Call Attention signal echoing from the signal box on the platform. Soon the level crossing gates would be wound across and three signals, Starter, Home and Distant, pulled off to herald the arrival of the train. This might be anything from a railcar or push-and-pull set to a rake of five or six

A tranquil scene at Oakamoor on the North Staffordshire Railway's Churnet Valley line about 1910

non-corridor coaches behind a 4-4-0 or tank locomotive. As the guard disposed of his newspapers, railway letters, perhaps an empty pigeon hamper or a refrigerated Eldorado ice cream container, the passengers would settle down on horsehair stuffed seats or replace the items he had unloaded with the produce they were taking to market. Station master and guard consult their watches, the latter whistles and waves his green flag, the porter at the front of the train relays the 'Right Away' signal and the driver eases the regulator open to take hold of his fairly easy load.

The market day journey itself would be fairly short and largely devoted to discussing the price of barley and eggs or the shortage of hay. The men would continue with farming matters at the stock or poultry market while the women filled their baskets with those special items which even the comprehensive shelves of the village store and post office did not stock. Some would take a substantial midday meal as a piece of self-indulgence to compensate for the daily tie of milking or the long hours of harvesting; others managed on one of those bowls of hot peas whose smell was almost irresistible. Fed, wiser and provisioned the farming families returned home in the late afternoon with the help of a railway that had done nothing remarkable, but had made its contribution to their lives and to the nation's business.

A luggage barrow and bowsers for replenishing coach water supplies

If the railway passenger service came to affect the lives of nearly everyone in the country, the impact of freight movement was even greater. The existence of a railway network able to distribute products the length and breadth of the land produced larger markets for existing goods, stimulated new ones, helped to reduce prices and created many ancillary demands in the process. The Liverpool and Manchester line was conceived as a freight railway but passenger receipts exceeded those from freight right from opening and the first goods train did not run until the end of 1830 when *Planet* hauled an 18 ton load from Liverpool to Manchester in under three hours including stops for water and oiling. Then, for over a hundred years starting around the middle of the last century, freight was worth more to railways than passengers until the situation changed again and the vulnerability of their freight business was to become the Achilles heel of the nationalised system.

With railway costs difficult to analyse back to the basic wagon load production unit and trade generally booming, railways soon moved away from the simple tariffs of the early years. The distance involved played some part but the main factors influencing the fixing of rates became the type of traffic involved and what the sender could afford to pay in relation to his own markets. The principle of 'charging what the traffic will bear' became commonplace and led to competing manufacturers having vastly different transport costs depending upon where they were located and the strength of the competition between the various lines and with canals and coastal shipping. This practice so offended the business interests of the time that legislation was ultimately forthcoming and required the railways to produce and publish maximum rates, increases in which could be challenged as unreasonable. Under these constraints the railway companies eventually found themselves unable to lift their freight earnings to match rises in working expenses. Already over-capitalised and bearing heavy interest burdens, the margins for shareholders and investment both diminished so that reinvestment was never as high as it should have been. Combined with the ravages of World War I these factors made the system vulnerable to road competition almost as soon as it began to emerge.

Many of the early tramways had been built to carry coal to fuel the fires of industry and the hearths of those who worked in it. The Stockton and Darlington Railway owed its existence to coal and that other member of the pioneer trio, the Canterbury and Whitstable Railway, listed as the first item in the 'Rates of the Company's Charges':

> Coal, at the Canterbury station, per chaldron, including landing at
> Whitstable . . . 4s 6d

Some of the coal moved in traditional sailing vessels to rivers, creeks and inlets
was siphoned away by the new railway lines but their main effect was to stimulate
the inland coalfields such as those of the Midlands and South Yorkshire. Soon
heavy coal trains were a regular sight on the rail network and although seaborne
coal in coastal vessels began to take second place from 1867 the shipping industry
began to feel the benefit when more and more lines brought coal down to the
seaport staithes for shipment oveseas. Areas like South Wales became
honeycombed with lines, independent companies running down the valleys,
Great Western Railway lines probing north from the east-west main line
through Newport, Cardiff and Swansea, and vassals of the Midland and London
and North Western Railway carrying out feats of incredible engineering to build
routes across the heads of the valleys and siphon off coal to their own routes or
ports.

Hand in hand coal and the railways transformed many areas of Great Britain.
In South Wales, Barry was just a modest coastal village until the enterprise of
David Davies of Llandinam conceived the idea of the Barry Docks and Railways
Company and opened a vast new port in 1889, feeding it with a new railway
which tapped the Ely, Rhondda, Taff, Cynon and Rhymney valleys. The export
of coal through Barry and the other South Wales ports reached a record level in
1913 when Cardiff alone dealt with 10 million tons, keeping its 54 coal hoists and
cranes at full stretch. When the Great Western Railway inherited these docks at
grouping it found itself with a vast area of one hundred and sixty-five acres
handling business of every kind, from the catch of the local fishermen and
imported ore for the steel industry to the vast quantities of export coal and
finished steel products. South Wales was an area that benefited early from
grouping rationalisation, the docks at Port Talbot being the first to tip the new 20
ton coal wagons in August 1924.

If the market day passengers of the last chapter had been standing at one of the
stations on the Great Northern and Great Eastern Joint Railway line and

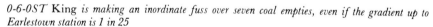

_0-6-0ST_ King _is making an inordinate fuss over seven coal empties, even if the gradient up to
Earlestown station is 1 in 25_

After the war 'Austerity' locomotives frequently handled the larger coal trains, as 90212 is doing from Parkside colliery, Newton-le-Willows

In addition to the larger collieries many smaller ones added their output to the rail network, perhaps using inclines like this one at Kilmersdon

waiting to take the train to Lincoln they would have been well aware of the importance of the railways' coal business. As early as 1834 the Grand Northern and Eastern Railway had planned a line to convey coal and merchandise from the North to London but it was August 1882 before its successor, the Great Eastern Railway, managed to avoid the need to exchange such traffic with the Great Northern Railway via Peterborough. After years of bickering between the

Standard Class 4 No 75030 assembles its train at Leek on the former North Staffordshire Railway in 1966

two companies agreement had been reached on the Great Northern and Great Eastern Joint route northwards from March via Spalding, Sleaford and Lincoln and soon heavy coal trains were heading south and passing long loads of empty wagons returning to the collieries.

There would be very few stations on the line itself which did not have a small coal merchants business based there, receiving two or three trucks a week, unloading every lump by shovel to stacks or sacks. The bigger merchants might have contracts to supply large users, but many sold all their coal in sacks to private homes or to local farmers who needed a few extra bags to feed the steam engine which hauled and powered the threshing rig at harvest time. All the coal had to be weighed and apart from such simple machines as a hand barrow-like platform on which a sack could be wound up to shoulder height for transfer to the rough cape across the coalman's back, all movements were made by the muscle power of the coalman or his delivery horse. At least the North Eastern Railway built raised staithes to allow bottom door discharge of coal wagons, but elsewhere it was a largely unmechanised business right up to the advent of coal concentration schemes.

To most railways coal was the single most important commodity. In an area like that served by the Great Northern and Great Eastern Joint Railway and the Great Eastern Railway agriculture was the other prime source of traffic so that 'fuel and food' dictated the railway freight traffic activities. The position changed slightly after the turn of the century when, on the Great Eastern Railway for example, factories began to appear in areas like the Lea Valley and served by the Cambridge main line. The Great Eastern Railway set out to cater

Haddenham, one of the smaller Cambridgeshire vegetable loading stations

for these new sources of traffic and in 1906 introduced vacuum brake fitted wagons to work on express freight services between Spitalfields (London) and Doncaster. Four 'Claud Hamilton' 4-4-0s were allocated to these workings which, by 1914, had built up business to the point where two 25-wagon trains were running each night at speeds producing an average of nearly 40mph. This tradition continued right up to the last years of the wagon load era, with 1945 offering such named freight trains as the *Lea Valley Enterprise* for fruit, flowers and light industrial traffic and the *Essex Enterprise* running from the Chelmsford area. These were followed, by the end of the decade, with plans to run sixteen Class 'C' express freight trains on an interval basis and dovetailed in with the passenger service but by this time the general freight business had become very vulnerable to road competition and British Railways were discovering the dividends of larger wagons and block train operation.

As the railway freight business grew the simple process of combining wagons into trains became infinitely more complicated as trains were remarshalled en route to maintain economic train sizes. The problems increased with the advent of road competition when speed first began to be important and industry came gradually to expect an overnight transit. The traditional loose-coupled train headed by an 0-6-0 locomotive and made up of open wagons with only hand brakes and with axles turning in a box packed with grease had to be bettered. The day of the express freight train 'fully fitted' with vacuum braked wagons — or, at least, with a fitted portion at the front and the remaining wagons 'piped' to carry the vacuum — had arrived. Many of these, like the fish and meat trains from Scotland to London, ran as through services but others needed shunting on the way and the mixture of traffics and services, coupled with demands for greater economy and efficiency, led to a new approach to intermediate marshalling.

On the outskirts of March, in the flat Fenland country of East Anglia, Britain's first fully mechanised marshalling yard was built at Whitemoor in the period from 1929 to 1933. It consisted of up and down yards on either side of the Great Northern and Great Eastern Joint Railway route, each provided with reception sidings, a raised 'hump', sorting sidings and a departure area. As each train arrived and released its engine to the nearby March locomotive shed, a shunter would record its wagons according to destination on a 'cut card', uncoupling behind each group for the same forward service as he did so. As the train was propelled at $1\frac{1}{2}$mph over the hump the 'cuts' would separate on the descending portion and be guided into the right sorting siding by a Shunter Switchboard Operator who had pre-set the electrically controlled points according to the information on the cut card. After their gravity separation wagons were slowed down by the use of hydraulic retarders which allowed a Shunter Retarder Operator to apply braking pressure on the wheel rims according to his assessment of the weight of the wagon, its speed and how far it had to run to join other wagons already in the sorting siding. One of the many yard pilot engines would then move a completed train down to the departure sidings ready for the onward train engine and crew.

The basic process was simple and effective. The up yard could handle 1,000 wagons a shift and the down yard included some fourteen thousand coal empties a week in its varied work pattern. Damage and delay were small in relation to the throughput but life got very hectic in the second half of the afternoon shift when fitted portions had to be made up for the nightly peak of fast freight departures. Exceptional items could be dealt with but were, inevitably, something of a nuisance. A load of apples from France might be in a ferry van with studded Mansell wheels and thus need to be hand braked for the retarders would sheer off the studs, livestock wagons had to be worked by a pilot to the feeding and watering point for animals could not be expected to take kindly to hump shunting, and any abnormal or out-of-gauge load could not be allowed to hurtle down the yard gradients for it was likely either to prove too much for the retarders or they might stop the wagon, leaving the load to be catapulted ahead!

The other feature of the Whitemoor complex was the small Norwood Yard which specialised in dealing with the urgent and non-routine flows of traffic, shunting them at speed in the conventional manner over a slightly raised 'knuckle'. The northern part of Cambridgeshire has long been noted for its fruit growing and Norwood Yard came into its own in the fruit season when the fourteen sidings might handle as many as 600 wagons between about 5.30pm and

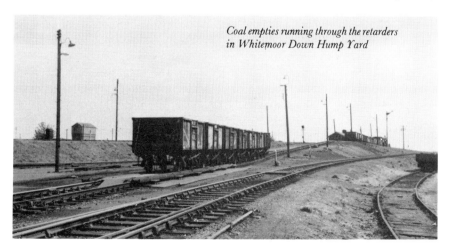

Coal empties running through the retarders in Whitemoor Down Hump Yard

8.30pm. The fruit growing area stretches from St Ives to Wisbech and in the season the process of picking starts soon after it is light. Right up to the 1960s the railway system handled a substantial volume of the business by freight and passenger train services and each year a special programme was drawn up to ensure adequate supplies of ventilated vans with extra trains to haul them. From late morning onwards railway lorries and those of the growers started bringing in boxes and crates of freshly picked produce to loading points on the St Ives and Wisbech branches and along the main lines towards Ely and Spalding.

Strawberries are a speciality of the area and the Wisbech and Upwell Tramway fed many van loads to Wisbech for onward movement to Whitemoor. The tramway, which followed a public road for the greater part of its length, was opened from Wisbech to Outwell on 20 August 1883 and on to Upwell on 8 September 1884. Until the beginning of 1928 a passenger service operated using special coaches with tramway-type gangways (one being used later in the film *The Titfield Thunderbolt*), but plans to extend the line through the streets of Wisbech to the market place were never carried out. The line served Elm Bridge, Boyce's Bridge, Outwell Basin, Outwell Village and Upwell and, until August 1955, was worked by a series of tram engines with working parts enclosed, warning bells and cow-catchers, and governors fitted to restrict the speed to 8mph. In the line's heyday up to six trains were run during the fruit season and three at other periods. There was even an office van vehicle which conveyed a clerk for each loading point so that he could start the process of documenting the hundreds of crates, boxes, bags and punnets. Sadly, the tramway closed in 1966.

Orders for vans for fruit loading were determined by the conditions obtaining in the markets and also by the performances of the rail services with the previous day's loadings. Additionally, all the growers wanted to go on picking as late as they could so vans were arriving at Whitemoor with very little time to spare before the departure of the trunk services to London, Southampton, Bristol, Liverpool, Manchester, Leeds, Sheffield, Nottingham, Newcastle and Hull. As soon as they were transferred from the arrival sidings to Norwood Yard trains would be shunted at remarkable speed with driver and shunter establishing an easy understanding and economical rhythm and wagon chasers using their brake sticks to slow the separated shunts at exactly the right point. As trains were formed they were engined and despatched to allow more loads in, and by the time the late shift finished at 10pm the day's crop would be on its way to the nation's table.

The railway system handled a great volume and variety of market traffic. While the fruit traffic was being loaded in Cambridgeshire, other areas dealt with large volumes of potatoes, peas, beans, sprouts, lettuce, tomatoes and other market garden produce. One busy growing area was that region of Bedfordshire surrounding the Great Northern main line from St Neots to Biggleswade. In fields and greenhouses village women picked feverishly while the market price was right and the produce was rushed in carts and lorries to the stations at St Neots, Tempsford, Sandy and Biggleswade and to the public freight siding at Langford.

Some vans went off to the provincial markets, others sped south to cater for the vast consumption of the London area. With other flows, like the rhubarb from

Yorkshire, special handling and cartage teams at King's Cross unloaded the arriving wagons early in the morning and fed their contents to the premises of the merchants at Covent Garden, Spitalfields and Borough Market. The railway agents helped delivery drivers to find a spot to unload and coped with the complications of market tolls and regulations and at Smithfield, at least, the process was completed with a hearty breakfast once all the Scotch beef had arrived, been sold and sent on its way to the butchers' slabs of the Home Counties.

The fish market for London has traditionally functioned at Billingsgate and this business clearly demonstrated the vital role of railways in the food distribution process. The smaller ports loaded their specialities, such as pilchards from Exmouth or shellfish from the Essex estuaries, and the larger ones the multiple wagon loads of herrings, cod, plaice and lesser fish. The herring fishing fleet followed the shoals down the East Coast from the Scottish ports to those of the Humber and East Anglia. With them came the fishergirls ready to smoke the freshly caught herrings into golden brown kippers. At the quays of Lossiemouth, Fraserburgh, Aberdeen, Hull, Grimsby, Yarmouth and Lowestoft the incoming trawlers and drifters would be quickly unloaded and the open crans and boxes auctioned, nailed down and transported to the railway sidings. The sights and sounds were unforgettable, rust-stained vessels littered with nets, tackle and the spillings of ice, salt and fish, the hectic and competitive process of selling, the smoking flames of the kipper stalls and the frantic loading and labelling of railway vans.

The railway system carried every type of food and food product. The grain harvest was either milled locally or carried by train to maltsters throughout the country, frequently with premises in railway yards. The best barley went north to the Scottish distilleries and Scotch seed potatoes came back across the border in return. As breweries grew large they demanded more truck loads of hops and as nourishment standards improved more and more churns of milk moved out of the pasturelands of the South West towards London and the Midlands. In the same direction went the Cornish broccoli crop while the ports of the Bristol Channel unloaded many tons of bananas, tea and other good things of life. Even the output of cavalry stables was moved by train to ensure that crops would be bigger and better and another colourful movement was that of the waste of the Yorkshire clothing mills, known as 'shoddy', which came south by the truckload

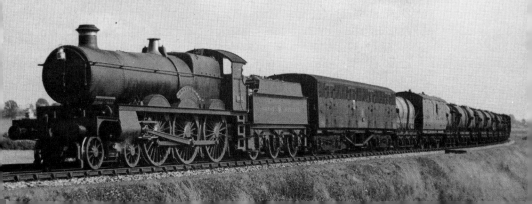

The Great Western Railway moved thousands of gallons of milk, initially in churns and later in six-wheel tanks of the sort here seen behind 4-6-0 Lady of the Lake

Milk churns being loaded at Paddington station during the 1926 General Strike

to be spread on the land in a pageant of mixed hues. At the other end of the pattern of the food and agricultural activity, railways moved vast quantities of tinned goods and frozen products. Among the latter were the huge sides of beef suspended from special van fitments and kept at a low temperature by the action of packs of dry ice provided at the beginning of the transit.

A specialised but widespread railway activity was the carriage of livestock. Prior to the coming of railways the animals had been moved on the hoof, along the old drove roads, taking days and losing weight in the process. From the pastures of Wales and the West sheep and cattle were driven across the southern counties to Sussex and Surrey, given a short time to fatten up and then sold and slaughtered to meet the appetites of such Londoners as could afford the luxury of meat meals. The new railways started to cater for this business early. Indeed, the Liverpool and Manchester Railway built wagons for the carriage of cattle and pigs well before the line opened for a 1929 report referred to them as being an improvement upon the vehicles used to carry human passengers a generation earlier. Within a year Irish pigs arriving by ship at Liverpool were being conveyed on to Manchester for 18d each and early Liverpool and Manchester prints depict several instances of livestock conveyance.

The steady growth in the consumer demand for meat led to increases in both livestock production and imports. The latter doubled in a decade as meat prices dropped from 60s to 40s per cwt at the turn of the century. In addition to its livestock wagons each railway company provided a raised loading dock at nearly all its stations and special pens at many. The movement regulations were also developed to a level of detail that would ensure safe and humane movement for the beasts themselves. Small and large animals were to be loaded separately, pigs kept from sheep or calves and bulls or other horned stock either tied at the head or neck or kept separate by the use of partitions. By law a cow could not be sent by rail if likely to calve en route and if the railway staff had doubts they were instructed to ask for a written assurance on the matter!

To avoid suffering, arrangements could be made for cows to be milked on the journey and wagon labels had to show both the time of loading and when feeding and watering was due. Sheep could go 36 hours without water, other animals 24 but, in practice, these maxima were related to what suitable facilities could be arranged on the journey. This was frequently an exchange point, possibly a marshalling yard, where special staff were provided and where all wagons conveying livestock were examined to ensure that there was no animal down or otherwise injured. If there was a vet would be called, and the owner contacted by telegraph if the beast was found to be mortally injured. If he was not available the unfortunate animal went off to the local butcher.

Washing down cattle pens after use was one of the mundane sides of the activity but it could have more hectic moments. In some instances animals have taken a dislike to rail travel and escaped from the prospect with their custodians in hot pursuit. In one case in Yorkshire a bull eluded the livestock wagon and its owner and had a few hours of glorious, rampaging freedom until the local Home Guard detachment ended the drama with a bit of firearms practice. However, most movements were straightforward and just part of one of the many railway involvements in the carriage of fuel and food.

OTHER FREIGHT FACILITIES
8

The railway freight business involved more than just serving mines and factories, farms and markets. Long after the first inroads had been made by road haulage it continued to provide the nation's industrial arteries and to sustain its consumer business — and, indeed, still contributes much today. This freight activity, at its peak, consisted of several separate businesses which treated the track and traction as common. The wagon load business was quite a different operation from that of conveying 'smalls', eg consignments weighing less than one ton and this, in turn, was quite dissimilar from the movement of merchandise by passenger train. Each of these businesses then had sub-divisions. There was a vast difference between the traffic of the steel industry, the intake of ore from Northamptonshire and limestone from Derbyshire and the despatch of ingots or finished products, and the requirements of the ports or the timber trade. The movement of a huge boiler bore little relation to the conveyance of a load of hides and skins or the clay requirements of the Staffordshire potteries. The smalls business could (and sometimes did!) mix cartons of butter with drums of lubricating oil and the traffic conveyed at passenger train rates could be as varied

Fowey in Cornwall had a passenger service from 1895 to 1965 but it has dealt with china clay (seen here in barrels destined for the Staffordshire Potteries) via Carne Point from 1869 and still does so, the route via Pinnock tunnel becoming an English China Clays roadway after closure

as a carton of live chicks conveyed in the guard's van or the bulk movement of newspapers and mails. Each of these movements, and others like them, called for special vehicles, special handling equipment and skills, and special regulations governing acceptance, conveyance and charging.

Until well into this century the main constituent of the railway wagon fleet was, essentially, a wooden body mounted on a short wheelbase metal frame. The body might be in the form of a closed van for carrying goods susceptible to the elements or theft, but more often the open sided wagon was used and this was the railways' main carrying workhorse for over a hundred years. With sides of varying heights it could be used to carry anything from machines to coal and, if

Paddington cartage vehicles around 1910 and loaded with every conceivable commodity

protection from the rain was required, a sheet could be placed over the load and tied down. Of some sixty thousand wagons owned by the London and North Western Railway at the end of the nineteenth century, mostly 15ft 6in long and 7ft 8in wide, only five thousand were vans. Well over half were ordinary open wagons and, of these, 60 per cent had sides of only 9in in height. With a carrying capacity of 7 tons, the basic materials were wrought iron for the underframes, cast iron for axle boxes and shoes and Bessemer steel for the wheel tyres and the axles themselves. Frames were of oak and the bodies of oak, teak or red pine.

The Great Western introduced 20-ton wagons for carrying locomotive coal in 1897, starting to fit oil instead of grease axle boxes in that same year. The fitting of

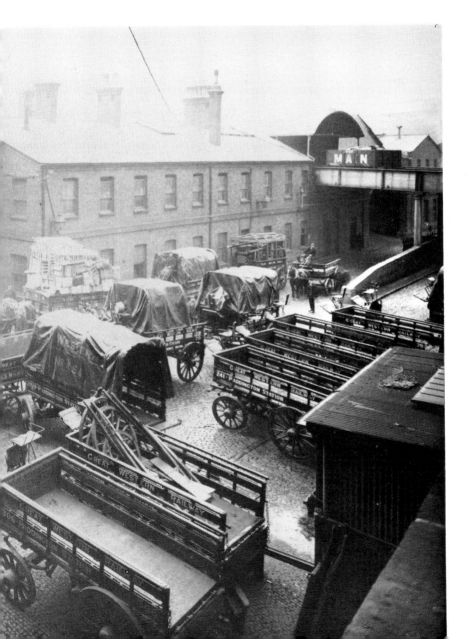

Shunting by capstan

vacuum brakes started in 1903 and two years later came a new build of 40-ton steel wagons for locomotive coal, at that time a very sizeable movement. Slowly the variety of wagons increased, coming to include well wagons for carrying motor vehicles, a number of designs for carrying machinery, refrigerated vans for meat, vans with steam heating, vans for bananas and even vans for gunpowder — the movement of which required an empty wagon to be placed either side of the loaded one. The war period stimulated the building of some big wagons and by the end of the 1920s each company had a few mammoth vehicles which could carry loads ranging up to 120 tons on four six-wheel bogies.

Up to World War II most 'exceptional loads' went by rail. Despite a normal width limit of 9ft 8in, the Great Western Railway came to the rescue by carrying an 11ft 2in diameter boiler which was put on rail at Pangbourne in 1913 after starting its journey from Staines to Oldbury by road and encountering such difficulties that the road haulier gave up. Later the company beat even this achievement by carrying a 45 ton generator which was 12ft 6in wide. The record went up to 14ft 4in in 1933 with the conveyance of a cylinder from Bury to Keynsham for installation in the factory of E.S. & A. Robinson. A 'Crocodile H' wagon was used, no trains were permitted on adjacent lines, very often the wrong line had to be used and to pass under some of the bridges the track itself had to be slewed to a central position.

The movement of these exceptional loads provides something of a picture of the sheer range of the railway freight activity on behalf of the nation's work and

Ex-Midland Railway 0-6-0 No 58224 (originally No 1615, built in 1883) hauling a goods train at Millers Dale station in 1955. There was considerable traffic in limestone from this station

leisure. One of the very long items conveyed by the Great Western was a steel mast moved from Liverpool to Millbay Docks, Plymouth. No less than 138ft long, it needed seven bolster wagons coupled together to support it. Another maritime movement was that of the two propellors for RMS *Mauretania*. The statuary group representing Charity, Justice and Foresight required movement from Frome to Piccadilly, London for the Norwich Union Insurance Society and the Great Western Railway specialists managed to arrange it, although Justice had to be beheaded temporarily to keep the consignment within gauge. The Captain Scott memorial at Devonport and the equestrian statue of General Buller at Exeter were other similar rail movements. Most impressive of all was the 'Crocodile L' wagon built in 1930 which had a capacity of 120 tons. It was built to carry stators and transformers for the electricity industry, the normal delivery method being for rails to be laid into the destination power station and the load jacked up to allow the carrying wagon to be withdrawn.

As the twentieth century progressed the railway companies developed an increasing range of wagons and actively encouraged customers to produce their own designs. The steel industry needed wagons for carrying long lengths of strip steel and wire and the construction industry wanted a long vehicle for conveying

Collecting milk from Ecton Creamery about 1920 on the narrow gauge Leek and Manifold Valley Light Railway. The milk tanks were standard gauge for the eventual journey to Finsbury Park, London, but were carried along the narrow gauge line on the special transporter wagons seen here. The creamery was housed in the former smelting works of the famous Ecton Copper Mine, whose waste tips are seen in the background

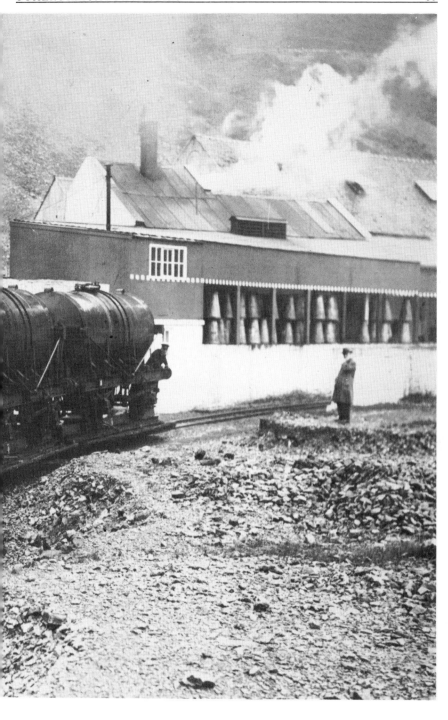

Kenyon Junction yard was used for marshalling coal trains from nearby collieries

One of the many locomotives used on the Ford Motor Company's private siding at Dagenham

bridge girders and similar items. To meet these needs the bogie bolster wagon evolved, its bogies allowing the long wagon to traverse most curves and four bolsters being provided to support the load. Four-wheeled single bolster wagons were used to support the overhang of long loads and flat 'plate' wagons were available for the carriage of steel plates and sheets. 'Tube' wagons were longer than average four-wheeled trucks and carried the pipes manufactured in the Midlands; by a curious coincidence, demonstrating the adaptability of the railways, such wagons were later used for the carriage of the modern, extruded plastic pipes which replaced the metal version.

Each company developed a number of special wagon designs to meet the needs of businesses peculiar to their own area. As the demand for milk grew and its conveyance in churns became increasingly uneconomic, milk tanks were built to bring thousands of gallons from the West of England to depots at West Ealing and Ilford. Similarly, as the dozens of small private brickyards south and east of

Peterborough were combined, first as Phorpres and then as part of the London Brick Company, the London and North Eastern Railway built all-steel bogie wagons for carrying their output. Later these were transferred to form trains for carrying London's refuse from a depot at Finsbury Park, known as 'The Vestry', to tips in Hertfordshire.

In this century, investment in private owners' wagons has been high. A pre-war coal train might exhibit the names of dozens of different collieries, merchants and factors, and large firms in other spheres — like Rowntrees and Colmans — invested in their own vans to add a splash of colour to the lines of grey, black or just dirty, wagons that made up most freight trains.

In addition to the facilities for acceptance and collection of goods at its conventional depots, the major railway companies would allow customers tenancies and encourage private sidings. The trader had to pay for the installation of his private link to the network, had to keep it up to the standard stipulated by the railway civil engineer and was frequently under commitment to sustain an agreed level of business. Some very large private siding networks came into being. Along the north bank of the Thames the upper reaches of the river were honeycombed by the dock lines which all became part of the Port of London Authority empire from 1909. Between the Authority's London Docks and those at Tilbury were other large networks such as that of the Ford Motor Company where delightful tank locomotives, resplendent in a green livery, moved around the plant positioning wagons transferred from the national system and transferring materials from one department to another in the Ford company's own wagons. Further down the estuary, timber, distribution, cement and other industries all had private sidings.

A whole industry was kept busy building industrial locomotives for use on such private systems, many of which also had their own wagon fleet. These could include wagons built specially, such as those used by the steel industry for the internal movement of hot metal and slag, or might just be trucks handed down from the main line companies. The latter were more likely on the group of light railways and small private lines which also transferred traffic to and from their bigger neighbours. Lines like the Wissington Light Railway transferred large quantities of agricultural produce to the main line system, but transfers from the Weston, Clevedon and Portishead Railway to the Great Western could be something of a liability and the latter was in the habit of insisting upon payment before supplying the wagons required by the smaller concern for loading.

In the difficult years following World War I the goods traffic of the newly grouped railways dropped steadily. In the ten years following grouping the total business of the London and North Eastern Railway group fell by 45 million tons. The process was halted at the beginning of the 'thirties when the 8 per cent drop in 1932 was followed by a 9 per cent increase in 1933, a trend which continued until 1938 when losses to road combined with difficulties in the steel industry to reverse the expansion. A feature of the uplift of this decade was the determined effort by the railways to resist the challenge of road, especially to their general merchandise business.

The resistance took several forms. Following the Road and Rail Traffic Act of 1933 the railway companies exercised their right as existing providers of

An LNER booklet countered the threat of competition from road transport in 1932:

LONDON AND NORTH EASTERN RAILWAY

E FFICIENT freight transport is vital to the community. Express Freight Services are vital to efficient freight transport.

The London and North Eastern Company have the pleasure to present these tables illustrating a number of the available express services, which only need to be known to be appreciated.

The tables indicate not only the due arrival times at destination, but also that which it is more important to know — the normal time at which merchandise is available for delivery. In many places this latter time is fixed by the requirements of the consignees, and the local trading practice.

The departure time from starting point is so arranged that, by high speed running throughout, the expresses may meet the trading needs at destination. Thus an early morning market at destination necessitates in some cases an early departure.

These early departure trains are amongst the finest freight services in the world, and their use is recommended not only for perishable traffic, but for all urgent merchandise suitable for loading in the express wagons.

An early start means an early delivery. There is no extra charge.

Great Western Railway goods train at Long Ashton

The same booklet gave a route map, departure times, and arrival times at the main destinations for both ordinary and market traffic for:

'The Three-Forty Scotsman'
the 3.40pm from King's Cross for seven principal Scottish destinations
'The Three-Fifty-Five Southerner'
the 3.55pm from Glasgow (High Street) for York, the West Riding, the GCR network and Luton
'The Four-Five North Eastern'
the 4.5pm from King's Cross for York and the North East
'The Five-Fifteen North Eastern'
the 5.15pm for the North East, also picking up at Sandy and Biggleswade
'The Six O'Clock West Riding'
the 6pm from King's Cross to the West Riding, again picking up market traffic from Sandy and Biggleswade
'The Nine-Fifty Manchester'
the 9.50pm from Marylebone to the main towns of the North West
'The Five-Twenty-Five Newcastle'
the 5.25pm from Liverpool (Huskisson) to the opposite coast
'The Five-Fifty-Five Lancastrian'
the 5.55pm from Newcastle and 8.40pm from Hull to the North West
'The Seven-Fifty-Five Burton' and 'The Ten-Fifty-Five Nottingham'
the 7.55pm and 10.55pm departures from Hull
'The Eight-Twenty Midlander'
the 8.20pm from Grimsby to the East Midlands

transport to object to applications for new or extended road licences. They also set about improving their services. The London and North Eastern Railway booklet quoted above had 2-8-0 No 384 as a cover picture, with most of the internal illustrations depicting that great LNER workhorse the K3 Mogul which had shown itself capable of handling anything from twenty passenger bogies to a heavy coal train. By the time the 1938 version of the same booklet appeared pride of place on the front cover had been taken by a V2, No 4771 *Green Arrow*. One of the original batch of five, and based at King's Cross, *Green Arrow* proved another Gresley success, efficient in performance and comfortable on the footplate, and gave its name to the whole class.

The Great Western, which was more romantic in its freight train naming — 'The Farmers Boy', 'The Carpet', 'The Northern Flash', 'The Mopper Up' and 'The Pasty' were just a few of the soubriquets — had made an early start on defending its business from the road vehicle by pioneering its own road feeder activities. Although the first developments were in 'motor-omnibus' services, often in place of the horse-drawn vehicles of subsidised coach proprietors, two motor services for the cartage of goods traffic were in operation in South Wales before World War I. Although the position had never been seriously challenged the railway companies had no statutory powers to operate road transport and the Great Western remedied this by obtaining the Great Western (Road Transport) Act of 1928. The Act was then put to good use in developing new omnibus companies in conjunction with existing operators and to develop country cartage arrangements.

GREAT WESTERN RAILWAY

Country Cartage Arrangements

T HE Great Western Railway have developed arrangements whereby the collection and delivery of merchandise and parcels traffic from and to shops, farms and private residences are undertaken within a radius of approximately 20 miles from over 160 stations on their system.

This pamphlet gives a list of the stations from which Lorry Services operate at the present time, together with particulars of the collection and delivery charges for goods and parcels.

A list of the villages served at least twice weekly by the various Country Lorry Services is also included which enables charges to be calculated throughout to destination. Collection from and delivery to other villages and premises not shewn in the list, within 20 miles of any of the lorry centres is also performed when occasion arises.

Special journeys are not undertaken for less than reasonable lorry loads and the scale for small consignments only applies where sufficient general traffic is available to justify the running of the lorry.

The map at the end of the book demonstrates that practically the whole of the country districts served by this Company are now covered by these special arrangements, which will be extended in other directions in due course.

By means of these Services consignors can be assured not only of expeditious rail conveyance but prompt delivery to their customers in outlying areas.

The utilisation of these Services by Farmers will release their lorries, horses and carts for more important work.

Where goods train traffic conveyed by rail at rates which include collection and delivery services within the usual boundary is dealt with by means of the Country Lorry Services, the road rates will be appropriately reduced.

The rates quoted in the pamphlet do not apply to heavy machinery or to articles of exceptional bulk in relation to weight such as agricultural implements, bales of feathers, light furniture, nor do they apply to such traffics as Household Removals, Live Stock, Milk, Coal or Bricks. For such special traffics, independent quotations will be made on application to the Goods Agent or Station Master.

The cartage of Milk is a regular feature, and as an indication of the rate the Company is prepared to charge for cartage of reasonable quantities it may be stated that up to 5 miles collection can generally be effected for $\frac{1}{2}$d per gallon, which includes the cartage of the empty churns.

The transport of Sugar Beet from Farm to Factory is undertaken. Special cartage arrangements are made and favourable rates quoted by Rail and/or Road to meet all requirements.

The Company is prepared to undertake the cartage of Live Stock to and from stations marked * as well as its throughout conveyance by road between farms and markets in the areas covered by the Country Lorry Services radiating from such stations. Details of charges and conditions can be obtained from the local goods agent or station master.

The Chief Goods Manager and Superintendent of the Line, Paddington Station, W.2, will be pleased to answer any enquiries in regard to Country Lorry Services arrangements as affecting Goods and Passenger Train Traffic respectively.

The Great Western Railway made special efforts to provide an integrated road/rail service.

The London and North Eastern Railway advertised a container service, as well as household and factory removals — they would even lay your carpets and hang your pictures!

▼

Containers

Road-rail containers provide door-to-door transport and enable economies to be effected in packing costs, both in respect of labour and materials. Risk of damage is minimised, the cost of returning empties is saved, and a speedier transit is ensured because of the elimination of intermediate handling.

Household Removals

The London and North Eastern Railway maintain a complete and efficient household removal service. A specially adapted container is sent to the house, into which experts carefully and securely pack the furniture and effects. The container is forwarded by express services to destination station and delivered to the new home, where the unpacking and placing in the house are again performed by experts. If desired, arrangements can be made for the laying of carpets and linoleum, hanging of pictures, placing of articles in cupboards and shelves, etc., to complete a really trouble-free removal.

A reduction of one-third rail fares to the new home station is made to members of the household when the furniture removal is carried out by the Company.

Works Removals

The London and North Eastern Railway undertake the movement of complete works, the scope of their undertaking, coupled with fast freight services, enabling them to effect the removal with efficiency and despatch. The comprehensive nature of the facilities provided by the Company is such as to ensure that transfer of Works can be carried out with the minimum of interference with business.

The Great Western and, indeed, the other companies also developed railhead distribution schemes. In the case of the Great Western Railway they offered railhead storage at selected centres with a delivery facility available over a radius of 30 miles so that participating firms could despatch in bulk to the storage point and then meet their customers' orders by using the railway vehicles for the final delivery.

In parallel with the investment in motor bus operation came the acquisition by the main line companies of the business complex of the Hay's Wharf Cartage Company which included the Carter Paterson and Pickfords operations. The latter was related to the railways' growing container activity to build up a facility, not only for household removals, but also for the movement of whole farms and factories. There was a steady expansion of container types, the 1 ton

Unloading from ship to wagon at Poplar Dock

Ferry wagons using the bridge linking ship and shore

'A' type and the larger 'B' types being supplemented by open, cage and other varieties, and the open wagons originally used for their conveyance were discarded in favour of specially-built container flats (Conflats), initially with chocks at intervals to cater for the varying container sizes and then with adjustable chocks. Station cranage facilities were improved to increase the number of stations able to lift containers.

Although the railway companies did not invest in local ancillary water transport in the same way that they did in road facilities, quite a significant volume of traffic was transferred to rail from docks and wharves and from barges. In the London docks traffic might be either transferred over the quays and incur one set of charges for the custom examination, handling and transfer to the main line system or pass over the ship's side and be moved by lighter to one of the railway depots with waterside quays, such as Poplar Dock or Brentford. Some very complex arrangements developed including the London, Tilbury and Southend Railway 'Guaranteed Tonnage' arrangement under which the railway offered favourable rates for the movement of Tilbury traffic to and from London, to enable Tilbury to compete with docks nearer London, and in return for a guaranteed level of business. Each flow tended to have its own special rates, often with quite complicated elements or conditions. Hides and skins moved for years from Tilbury to Moorlands of Glastonbury and many an argument took place over what load could be achieved in the traditional box van, the railway and trader wanting the maximum weight to be crammed in but the dockers having no easy task when it came to manoeuvring damp and heavy hides in the confined space available.

At the railway's own riverside depots a complex system of charging existed to cater for the wide range of traffics, operations and parties involved. At Poplar Dock the North London Railway charged other companies $1\frac{1}{2}$d a ton for the use of the North London Railway cranes in discharging grain, cement, rails and similar traffic from ship or barge to truck, adding another $1\frac{1}{2}$d per ton if a grab was used or increasing the figure to 3d if the traffic was hay, sleepers, timber or bricks. The handwritten book of regulations recording this added that if the other companies wanted to work outside the depot's normal hours of 6am to 6pm 'they must provide their own capstanmen' and that a North London Dock Foreman was 'to be on duty in any case.' An adjoining regulation, deriving from Board Minute 9727 records that on seaborne coal sent by Stephenson Clarke & Co to Poplar Dock a rebate of 3d per ton was to be allowed on traffic reforwarded by rail. From 1 July 1899 the rebate was increased to $4\frac{1}{2}$d on tonnage over 20,000.

Some traffic was transferred from canal to rail and considerable rail business was at one period derived from barges operating on the waterways of East Anglia. This business was brought under one of the inter-company 'pooling' arrangements under which traffic which would normally be the subject of fierce canvassing competition was allowed to follow its natural routings with the railways concerned sharing the receipts according to the share they had taken in a base period. There were twelve 'pools' in operation when the London and North Eastern Railway examined the Fen District Pool in 1928 and these included a Highland Livestock Pool, a Birmingham Iron and Steel Pool, a

An LNER report in 1928 on the decline in East Anglian barge traffic:

FEN DISTRICT POOL

The whole of the waterways which were in use for the lighterage of traffic prior to the institution of the Fen pooling arrangement are still navigable, though not in such good condition as previously, but very little boatage is now performed except by barges owned by the Beet Sugar Factories for the transport of beet. The Ely Sugar Factory have a fleet of between 100 and 150 barges and tugs, and the Wissington Factory a much smaller number.

In the vicinity of HOLME the Midland Level Drainage Commissioners do not consider navigation a primary consideration and the water level is so low that during the past two or three years traffic has not been boated to Holme Wharf in appreciable quantities, though we get it both by road and by boat at St Mary's.

At RAMSEY NORTH very little traffic is boated for either local mills or rail transit.

At PETERBOROUGH the same remarks apply, viz: that barging of traffic over the waterways is on the decline. We closed our Peterboro' Water Wharf during the war and filled up the water basin. The L.M.S. Co still have a steam crane at Peterborough East and do a little water business but nothing like what was done in the old days.

Looking at the question generally, and bearing in mind the fact that roads in country districts are now in much better condition, whilst many farmers possess motor lorries of their own and there are also many road motor haulage companies in existence, it seems to us that the fear of water competition is nothing like the same as in 1902, our principal enemy now being road transport.

Although the L.M.S. Co. are pretty keen in canvassing, we are of the opinion that we can hold our own assuming that no irregular tactics were adopted by them and that if there was open canvassing they were not allowed to charge less than the throughout rail rate from the station nearest point of origin, or permitted to sink any barging or cartage charges.

We take it that, bearing in mind the financial position of the railways, the Rates Tribunal would not agree (in the event of the Fen pools being withdrawn) to any irregular tactics being adopted by the L.M.S. which would put them in anything like the same position as previously, because this would be giving undue preference and would be distinctly opposed to the principle of fair competitive methods.

The L.M.S. Co. have undoubtedly reaped (at our expense) an extraordinary benefit from the pooling arrangements, having been paid considerable sums for doing nothing.

As the loss to the L.N.E. in connection with the Fen District pools is so excessive (£80,000 in five years), we strongly recommend that the pooling arrangement be cancelled, and we are of the opinion that if we are given a fair field we can hold our own in our respective districts against L.M.S. competition.

Tan-y-Bwlch on the Ffestiniog Railway early this century with both passenger coaches and empty slate wagons

The huge sundries goods depot at Bristol Temple Meads. The station layout has been remodelled since this picture was taken and the Bristol MAS panel box built, but the small signal box in the centre can still be seen

Liverpool Timber Pool and a Norfolk and Suffolk Goods Pool. The overall benefits were adjudged to be worthwhile but the report of the local District Managers at Peterborough and Cambridge to the Goods Manager at King's Cross shed an interesting light on the decline in barging and on relations between the LNER and LMS companies.

The efforts of the railways to provide a comprehensive and competitive freight service led them into all sorts of supplementary activities, many of which must have been more trouble than they were worth. In the days when grain was harvested by horse-drawn binder and then stacked to await the arrival of the contractor's agricultural engine and threshing rig, much of the final output went to millers and distillers by rail. To secure the movement to their route, each of the major railways offered grain sacks for hire, providing them long before the harvest had been gathered and making only a nominal charge provided the grain did eventually go by rail. The activity grew quite large, and on the London and North Eastern Railway a Sack Superintendent at Lincoln had a large staff to control the purchasing, supply and repair of the thousands of sacks owned by the company. Needless to say the system never quite worked as it was intended to and farmers not infrequently put sacks to other uses than loading them with grain. Some got forgotten for months and were returned needing the attention of the repairers, many a London, Midland and Scottish sack was loaded at a Great Western Railway station, and some never got accounted for at all.

As a result of all this attention to services and facilities, the main line companies remained significant carriers of freight until well after World War II. In the '30s the railways were involved in nearly every industry. The Great Western Railway, for example, carried products as diverse as china clay from Cornwall and gloves from Yeovil. In Bristol seven thousand people were employed in the tobacco trade, their labours producing up to five thousand packages a day for which the railway provided twenty-five to thirty vans to go to destinations all over the country. Temple Meads goods depot handled over 5 million

Sankey Viaduct with a 3F 0-6-0 just visible shunting on top

London Midland and Scottish Railway Company.	Summary of * _Foreign_ GOODS. E.R.O. 4654									
(_Midland_ Section).	**RECEIVED**									
Month of _October_ 19 _.._	At _SUTTON PARK_ Station.									

From STATIONS as below:—	Route.	No. of Inaccuracy.	Collected.		Delivered.		Collected and Delivered.		Not Carted.		Paid ons and Overcharges.			Paid.			To Pay.		
			T.	C.	T.	C.	T.	C.	T.	C.	£	s.	d.	£	s.	d.	£	s.	d.
G.W.																			
Bristol	Bristol						1									11			
Gosport	Vindly	✓					9							1	3	1			
Malvern Link	Wells		✓				1										—	0		
St Ives (Cornwall)	Bristol	✓					4							1	9	8			
Southall	Cal. + Jun						2				8	5		4	10		9	—	
Southam Road Halt	Lnds						20	2	✓		6	7	8						
Stratford on Avon	"						1		✓			1	5						
Laurie	Laurie			✓					✓			1	8						
Witney (Ger.)	"Ld.								✓	19	6			8		9	0.		
Wolverhampton	...						1		✓			1	4						
TOTALS...			1		19		20	2	1	19	6	8	1	9	2	19	7		

Certified as correctly compiled from the Abstract Totals, and that the additions of Abstracts and Summaries have been checked.

Signature _____ Agent.

All the Great Western stations listed as sending goods sundries to Sutton Park London, Midland and Scottish were 'Foreign' so far as that company's Goods Summary Form was concerned

consignments annually, including the smaller forwardings of the metal, engineering, aircraft, soap, brush and flour-milling activities which kept another fifteen thousand people in jobs. The railway also carried six hundred thousand tons of stone annually, moved thirty thousand tons of broccoli east from Cornwall and unloaded ten thousand tons of early potatoes and twelve thousand tons of tomatoes over the quays at Weymouth. It served the paper-making industry around Exeter, the milk condensing factory and electrical engineering works at Chippenham and the bacon-curing premises at Calne. Jam from Gloucester, china, shoes and sauce from Worcester, carpets, salt and canning from the surrounding area, flour from Birkenhead, soap from Port Sunlight, margarine from Bromborough and every imaginable type of product from the Birmingham area, all used trains to get to their final markets.

A picture of all this varied activity emerges from the books of instruction which the companies issued. A London, Midland and Scottish edition of 1931 runs to 92 pages nicely bound and detailing 283 instructions ranging from advice on the loading of poisons to the recording and quotation of rates. Warnings to pass agricultural engines or similar machines under the loading gauge is a reminder that the gauge of each company varied and that the agent's prospects would suffer a considerable reversal if a machine were to foul a tunnel during its journey. Sheets, ropes, chains and scotches all had to be properly stored and recorded and goods yard cranes and slings had to be inspected at regular intervals and a record of such inspections kept. The railway would undertake labelling, warehousing and bonding services and had a complicated set of charges for these and other additional services.

The attitudes of the period are revealed in some of the general instructions issued to the LMS company's agents in 1931:

Station working expenses	**27.** Agents must keep the working expenses of their stations at the lowest point consistent with efficiency and the requirements of the traffic.
Stores, &c., to be economised	**28.** Agents must exercise a strict supervision over the use of all stores, stationery, water, lighting and power, also grain sacks, sheets, ropes, hampers and cloths, and the Company's property generally, and must impress upon their Staffs the necessity of exercising economy and preventing waste of any kind.
Increase of traffic receipts	**29.** An important duty is to endeavour to increase the traffic receipts. This can best be accomplished by civility and attention to traders; by facilitating the collection, forwarding or delivery of traffic; by promptitude in attending to and redressing complaints; by attention to correspondence, and by correctness and regularity in dealing with the public.

Agents should keep in touch with the traffic in their district and bring to the notice of the traders the numerous facilities afforded by the Company; communicate with Headquarters when traffic which could be carried by the Railway Companies is being, or is likely to be, conveyed by alternative competitive means, give suggestions as to rates and train alterations for better cultivation and working of traffic, and use every endeavour to secure new and increased traffic.

Any new competition adversely affecting the interests of the Railway Companies must be reported.

PASSENGER FARES & FACILITIES

9

The range of fares offered by the railway companies did much more than cater for the general travel requirements of the community and help it to enjoy its leisure. Right from the beginning the system was expected to shoulder some social responsibilities and the concessions widened until they covered not only the disadvantaged and such obvious groups as the police and armed forces but also became part of the economic fabric of the nation in forms as diverse as workmens' fares and special facilities for commercial travellers.

The contribution made by the railway system in two world wars was vast and does not need re-stating here. Extensive use was also made of the railways in peacetime for moving personnel from one posting to another, for duty journeys and for soldiers, sailors and airmen going on leave. The warrants provided by each branch of the services were exchanged for tickets at the railway booking office and then used by the companies as the basis for reclaiming the money involved. The railways also issued 'Furlough' tickets to soldiers, sailors and airmen travelling for their own purposes. These provided a reduced rate ticket for the person concerned and, since pay for the ranks was reckoned in terms of shillings and pence until the middle of the century, were doubtless a welcome privilege. Many other facilities were also provided to meet the needs of HM

The army camp at Ludgershall became about the busiest point on the Midland and South Western Junction line

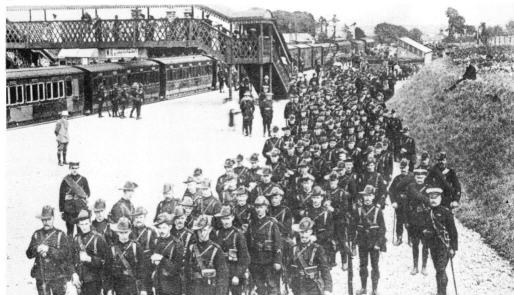

Forces, including such provisions as allowing dog handlers and couriers with special documents or stores to travel in the guard's van.

Disabled ex-servicemen and other bona fide victims of enemy action were part of the railways' considerable connection with the disadvantaged in the community. Wheelchairs, for example, were parked, stored or carried free. There were special arrangements for the blind, their attendants and guide dogs, and the railways went to endless trouble to liaise with hospital and ambulance services. Not only were some coaches built with special windows to take stretcher cases but a whole train formation might be remarshalled to make sure one of these was provided on the train which the Red Cross arranger might wish to use. There was also a very comprehensive disinfecting process for use after the conveyance of those suffering with infectious or contagious diseases.

In the middle years of the eighteenth century there were dramatic increases in building in many British towns and cities. In London the dock building period was followed by that of many of the capital's railways, all consuming vast quantities of land which in the inner area had been occupied by the mean and crowded homes of the poorer section of the community. Railway enabling Acts might contain provisions requiring the offer of cheap fares as a compensation but the theory that people would thus move out to more spacious areas and a better standard of home worked initially only in respect of the middle and upper classes. However, helped by general improvements in working conditions and wages, and by the positive approach to commuter traffic of railways like the Great Eastern — 'the workman's London railway' — ordinary people increasingly moved out of the inner city.

The Cheap Trains Act reinforced the powers of the Board of Trade and the Railway Commissioners to insist upon adequate accommodation 'for workmen

A view of Paddington between the wars with plenty of passengers waiting for the empty coaches just pulling into Platform 1. Much has changed since, but the 'Hairdressing Rooms' at least have survived

Refreshment trolley, now ready for a new lease of life with the Dean Forest Railway Society

Luggage barrows and a typical platform weighing machine for parcels traffic

going to and returning from their work at such fares and at such times between 6pm and 8am as appear to the Board of Trade to be reasonable and necessary'. By the beginning of the 1900s half the GER London arrivals were carried in workmens' trains or at the reduced fares available for clerks. Those travelling at more leisurely hours could take advantage of the season ticket facility, first recognised by the Liverpool and Manchester Railway as a way of securing regular business, of getting payment in advance and of reducing ticket queues. Some companies offered season tickets free for a period as an inducement to move out to the suburbs — and thus become dependent on rail travel — and many of the London area lines made special efforts to stimulate suburban business.

In 1912 the London, Brighton and South Coast Railway started its morning service of workmens' trains with a 4.30am from Coulsdon to London Bridge. A 4.40am left London Bridge for Purley and the East London line started the day with a 4.42am departure from New Cross which got to Whitechapel at 4.56am and Shoreditch at 4.58am, returning from the latter at 5.05am. Fares were very modest, 2d from South Bermondsey to London Bridge up to a maximum of 9d from Epsom. To qualify for a 'Cheap Working Class Ticket' the journey had to be completed by 8am and the company's conditions of issue stated:

> THESE WORKING CLASS TICKETS are issued at a REDUCED RATE, and in consideration thereof, are accepted by the Passenger on the express condition that the liability of the Companies to make compensation for injury, or otherwise, in respect of the passengers, shall be limited to a sum not exceeding ONE HUNDRED POUNDS . . .

Continuing its interest in developing its suburban services for the London commuter, the Great Eastern Railway followed the end of World War I with a study of how to cater for this business. The level of traffic at Liverpool Street was only exceeded at London Bridge but the fares paid by the short distance travellers would not have serviced the capital required for electrification. To solve this dilemma the Great Eastern introduced its 'Jazz' service on 12 July 1920, increasing train capacity, remodelling the layout at Liverpool Street and altering the train working methods to enable train turnrounds to be cut to under five minutes. Liverpool Street remains busy today but does not have quite the same atmosphere as that of the 'Jazz' era. In the busiest hours some forty thousand passengers would alight from or board the sets of four-wheeled coaches. No sooner had a train arrived from Enfield, Chingford, Palace Gates or the Broxbourne line than the crowds would surge out through the ticket barriers and the engine for the outward service would set back from its spur at the end of the platform. As it was coupled up and the platform indicators changed a new load of passengers was assembling to board, although arrivals far exceeded outward journeys in the morning and vice versa in the evening. With everyone loaded, brake and steam pipes coupled and the guard having changed ends the train would set off back for the suburbs, the released engine would follow it out to take its place in the spur and a new arrival would come charging in. On the opposite side of the station a similar process was taking place with trains from the Brentwood, Ongar and Loughton lines and the railway still managed to fit in its longer distance services on the Cambridge and Ipswich main lines.

Those travelling on many of the sub-standard fares were not entitled to take luggage with them, but for the majority of passengers on longer journeys luggage was an essential part of the journey process. It had been the custom on the stage coaches of the road era to carry a limited amount of luggage without additional charge, an element in the fare being assumed to cover this. The practice was inherited by the young railways and usually confirmed in the enabling Act, the free allowance coming to be something around 150lb for first class passengers and 100lb for those travelling third class.

In fact, luggage proved to be a vast and complex part of the railway activity demanding porters to carry it, racks and vans to house it on the journey and special charges for excess amounts or services like registration or collection and delivery. The early railways seemed to lose or run over a lot of it and this, coupled with the fact that they did not really enjoy carrying it free, frequently led to litigation. Matters were not improved by the fact that under the 1830 Carriers Act railways were liable, as insurers, for the safety of luggage and there were many wrangles over the definition of what constituted the personal luggage they were obliged to carry free. The accepted understanding was that such luggage must be for a passenger's 'personal use and convenience according to the habits of the class of life to which he belongs', so that when the Midland Railway charged a Mr Hudson 2s 6d for a child's rocking horse he brought back from London to Nottingham the railway was able successfully to defend its action when the gentleman took them to court in 1869.

Many passengers wanted to leave packages at a station for later collection and all but the smallest location offered 'Cloakroom' facilities. In a detailed list of charges for this service the railways differentiated between a tuck box and a violincello and charged twice as much for a pair of oars as they did for a Lacrosse stick. With the dripping brown glue so favoured by railway offices, a numbered counterfoil would be stuck on the deposited article and the main ticket portion handed to the passenger for use when the item was collected. A surprising volume of this 'Left Luggage' was not reclaimed and would eventually resurface at one of the railways' sales of lost property, unclaimed goods and similar abandoned commodities. Even if you bought nothing there, attending one of these sales was a

Busy scene at Waterloo in 1912

worthwhile experience even if only to marvel at the variety of things people left on trains or on deposit and then, apparently, forgot all about.

Simple everyday things like perambulators showed up the complexity of the sphere of adjuncts to railway travel. It was not permitted to take a 'hard' detachable body into a train compartment, only a soft one. If the latter contained a child it might be placed upon the seat of a compartment but, should a fare paying passenger wish to occupy that seat 'the owner (of the pram and contents), if NOT in possession of a travel ticket for the infant, should be tactfully asked to remove the carrier'. Since prams could also be the subject of a season ticket, or be delivered in London or even to the Western Isles, and there were just as many rates and regulations for dogs, bicycles and the other impedimenta of travel, it is little wonder that most of the railway books of instructions weighed at least four or five pounds!

A great deal of holiday luggage was forwarded under the 'Passengers Luggage in Advance' scheme. This recognised that the passenger would have been able to take his luggage with him, free, had he wished and offered the facility of carrying it before the journey at a nominal fee to cover the service of collection and/or delivery. Under the scheme a road vehicle would collect the luggage and have it waiting at the traveller's destination so that he could enjoy a relaxed, unencumbered journey. This saved the complications of seeking a porter, perhaps the most unjustly but most frequently criticised group of railway employees. Many conveyed huge mounds of luggage and saw their passengers safely seated with little or no reward beyond their normal wages, but those who put 'weazelling' (ie seeking tips) before their proper duties brought the activity into disrepute as they developed an eye for the best paying clients and wheeled their luggage barrows at all who threatened to get in the way. For many years official, licensed 'extras' were used at some of the bigger stations where other less official practices also crept in. At King's Cross for example one of the railway hangers-on marshalled the taxi movements and reputedly received a penny a call for his trouble.

Typical ordinary luggage labels

G.W.R.

Wolverhampton

VIA YATE & STAN JCT.

G. E. R.

From_____

TO

MALDON EAST

Most of the big country boarding schools used the railways to receive their pupils at the beginning of term and to dispose of them, thankfully, at the end. On such occasions as the latter, mounds of luggage would have to be collected by road vehicle and taken to the local station for labelling until the sixth former whose luggage had survived his school years could display it almost covered by the remnants of PLA labels, labels stipulating 'Shrewsbury via Crewe' or even, if he had managed some prestige journeys in addition, highly-coloured labels boasting of travel on 'The Broadsman' or some other named train. If the poor clerk on duty when the luggage lorry arrived had to cope with this in addition to the normal spread of business he would be very busy indeed and end up tired from lifting, cramped from scribbling and sticky from pasting.

A great deal was expected of the railway staff dealing with passenger fares and facilities. In addition to the routine business, those working in booking offices had to be prepared for the many exceptional circumstances for which each railway seemed to provide in abundance. The problem was not so much remembering the facility as the conditions which went with it. Single fare for the return journey would readily be offered to 'Grooms of Volunteer Officers', members of the 'Volunteer Sergeants' Tactical Association' travelling to take part in 'War Games', and even members of 'bona fide Civilian Rifle Clubs affiliated to the National Rifle Association, when travelling for rifle practice at the ordinary ranges of their Clubs'. The regulations offered single fare and a quarter for the double journey of 'Firemen in Uniform', adding the fascinating rider in brackets 'with or without their Fire Engines and Horse'. Boat crews attending regattas could have the same facility, but the validity of the ticket was a more complicated matter:

> . . . available from a week before to a week after the respective Regattas, the latter time being reckoned up to the time of starting on the return journey; the usual travelling time, as with a single journey ticket, is allowed in addition to the week for the return journey, which, however, must be commenced not later than a week after the Regatta.

Generally speaking the 1921-3 grouping simplified matters, but prior to that many of the fares and facilities reflected the state of the multi-company network and relationships. On most lines the validity of an ordinary single ticket or the outward half of a return ticket was on the day of issue only but tickets issued from Great Central Railway stations to the South Eastern, South Western, LBSC and LNWR areas were available for four days and those to Scottish lines for six. The same company warned, 'Passengers holding second class tickets issued by the L&Y and L&NW Companies are hereby informed that they are only available in the Third Class carriages of the GC Company's Trains' — where the standards would probably have been just as good anyway.

The Great Central also issued market tickets to no less than twenty-seven places, some on one day of the week, others on two. To Lincoln alone this facility applied from thirty-seven stations, one of them being Hull from which there were steamer departures at 5.30am and 9.15am and the option of travelling third class plus first class cabin or saloon. Some of these tickets were not available by corridor trains, others not available by express trains. In the same era before

In the days of wide streets and little traffic. The solid tyred Great Western Railway bus has brakes acting on the tyre itself and carries a board 'Great Western Railway Station and Wyke Regis'.

The inter-company rivalry shows up again in the Great Central Railway's notices regarding the facility for 'Through Carriages, Saloon, Family, and Invalid Carriages':

These Carriages, upon 24 hours' notice, can be sent to any part of the Line.

(a) **Through Carriages,** other than those named below, will be provided on the following Ordinary or Tourist fares being paid, viz.:-

    Six 1st Class fares, or

    Ten 3rd class fares, or

    Three 1st class and Four 3rd class fares

(b) For the use of a **Saloon or Family or Invalid Carriage** (but not for a Composite or any other Through Carriage reserved for the exclusive use of one party). Ordinary or Tourist Fares equivalent in amount to not less than Four 1st class and Four 3rd class tickets will be charged as a minimum. Each person travelling must, however, pay the fare for the class of Carriage used. This clause does not apply to 3rd class Saloon Carriages, the through-carriage arrangement, vide clause (a), applying thereto.

If the Passengers are proceeding to any Station on or over the *London Brighton and South Coast* or *South Eastern and Chatham Railways,* and are desirous of being booked through, fares equivalent in amount to not less than *seven 1st class* (five of which tickets must be 1st class) will be charged as a minimum in the case of Through Saloons or Family Carriages; they may, however, if they prefer it, be booked to London in accordance with clauses (a) and (b).

For the use of a through Family, Saloon, or Invalid Carriage conveying Passengers to stations on the *South Eastern and Chatham Line,* an additional charge of 20s over and above the passenger fares will be made.

A similar charge will be made to *London, Brighton and South Coast* Stations, except those competitive with the *London and South Western Company.*

World War I the railway booking clerk might be asked about coaches and omnibuses running in connection with his company's trains. The same Great Central Railway clerk who had booked the regatta crews or the market tickets could reasonably be expected to know that an omnibus met all trains at Kirton Lindsey to 'convey passengers to any part of the town' or that at New Holland two covered wagonettes met certain trains and carried passengers on to Barton on Humber and that, failing this, a trap might be hired at the Yarboro' Hotel, two minutes walk from the station.

A later booking clerk on the Great Western Railway would have to be just as knowledgeable for although grouping increased standardisation, it also led to a wider range of activities. He would have had a market fares range to handle and would also need to know that 'Passengers holding Market Tickets travelling without Personal Luggage may carry with them 60lbs of Marketing Goods, at Owner's Risk, Free of Charge.' He might also have to advise an intending third class traveller to Ireland, holding a Weekend Ticket, that if he wished to use the saloon on the Fishguard-Rosslare sailing he might do so 'provided there is accommodation and other circumstances permit, at the discretion of the Company, on payment of 5s 6d Single and 7s 6d Return.' This paragon of employees might also have to advise on the 'Romantic Dartmoor' trips which offered a scenic circular tour by 'Road Motor Observation Car' from Torbay. By the time the poor, harassed Great Western Railway employee had absorbed all these facilities, plus schemes for business travel, runabout tickets and the host of one-off excursions which kept his racks filled with handbills, it is hardly a matter for envy if the tea mug stains on the booking office table should testify to quieter moments in the life of a station.

Although these days road coaches are becoming more and more luxurious the trappings of road travel are never likely to quite equal those of a rail journey. The British station has always been a complex place and never more so than in the 'thirties when so much seemed to be needed to keep the passengers happy.

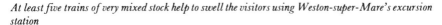

At least five trains of very mixed stock help to swell the visitors using Weston-super-Mare's excursion station

Excursions to Dartmoor by motor bus were part of the service offered to holiday makers by the GWR:

Romantic Dartmoor, via Chagford
EXCURSION TICKETS — will be issued each WEEK DAY as under —
Rail to Moretonhampstead
Road Motor Moretonhampstead to Chagford
Coach, Chagford to Moors and back
Road Motor Chagford to Moretonhampstead
Home by Rail from Moretonhampstead

ITINERARY OF COACH DRIVES

(BOX SEATS 1s EXTRA, to be paid to the Coach Proprietor,
Mr J.U. Winkfield, at Chagford.)

The Coach leaves the Globe Hotel, Chagford, shortly after arrival of the Road Motor Car.

MONDAYS AND THURSDAYS — To Grimspound and Postbridge, passing Bector Cross and Hookner Tor, embracing the very heart of Dartmoor, and commanding a splendid view of Princetown, halting at Grimspound to enable visitors to see the remains of the ancient hut circles, and other interesting relics of a bygone age, through the Challacombe Valley to Postbridge for lunch, returning by Warren Inn, Jurston and Meldon Hill, Chagford being reached about 5.15pm.

TUESDAYS AND FRIDAYS — Haytor by Meldon Hill, Beetor and Heatree Cross, Jay's Grave and Hound Tor — Bagtor with Saddle Tor and Rippon Tor in the distance — to Haytor Rocks, halting there 1½ hours, returning by the Terrace Drive, overlooking a vast stretch of land and sea, to Becky Falls and Manaton, arriving at Chagford about 5.15pm.

WEDNESDAYS AND SATURDAYS — To Widecombe-in-the-Moor and Grimspound, passing Honey Bag Tor, Hound Tor, Saddle Tor and Haytor Rocks, halting at Widecombe for 1½ hours; thence along a private road to the ancient British Village of Grimspound and Hookner Tor, whence is obtained a commanding view of some of the finest Tors on the Moors, with Princetown Prison in the distance. The journey will then be resumed through wild and romantic scenery over Stinial Down and Middle Down to Chagford, arriving there about 5.15pm.

Externally it presented a degree of grandeur closely related to the financial position and community aspirations of those who originally built it and to the sympathy of later architects who altered it to reflect changing traffic needs or compensate for the ravages of time. Country stations frequently combined a long approach road with a quiet dignity of style but larger stations might be as grand as St Pancras, Shrewsbury or Norwich or as plain as Salisbury or Preston. Their pretensions were usually extended to the hall or concourse, quite frequently panelled in expensive woods or marble from which peeped the tiny booking office windows with the simple wooden barrier, polished by generations of

Dirt platforms, oil lamps, simple shelters and a name board at Pantyscallog, but the train will be well patronised

waiting elbows, one of the institutions which shaped our national propensity to queue.

Adjacent to the ticket barrier would stand a tall red platform ticket machine with a narrow glass panel revealing it well stocked with 1d pasteboards and a shiny brass handle to pull once the penny had been inserted and dropped through its mechanical labyrinth to the metal drawer which the clerks emptied periodically. This was only the forerunner of other machine attractions which, for the magic penny, would dispense a bar of Nestle's chocolate, offer a pack of butterscotch or provide a weighing machine to repent on. Later, stations acquired those stubby contraptions which enabled you to spell out your name, or print 'No Hawkers, No Circulars' for your front gate, on a metal strip by moving a clock hand-like point round to the letters in succession and punctuating this process by pulling down the lever which did the imprinting.

For those already hungry or thirsty the refreshment rooms dispensed anything from rock cakes — on pedestal stands beneath a glass dome — to full meals with heavy polished cutlery and crockery bearing the company's crest. If a glass of stout was more to your taste you could receive it over the marble counter and then watch the trolley wheeled out to dispense tea to those unfortunate travellers whose train did not have a refreshment facility. Other staff carried their wares in baskets or offered reading material from the bookstall. In the waiting rooms horse-hair seats and huge fireplaces were relieved by a choice of pictures, something a little more restrained than the enamel pressures to buy Bovril or Pears Soap which competed with the railway posters on the walls outside. Subtly they called upon you to travel again, a message repeated by the sepia prints of the carriages when at last the much-anticipated moment of the train journey actually began.

SMALL AND SPECIAL TRAFFIC
10

Although railways have always earned most of their income from carrying passengers and the bulk products of industry, the many small and special consignments moved have represented useful additional earnings from costs which would largely have been incurred anyway. The extra van load of small consignments attached to a freight train would hardly alter its running costs and carrying parcels in the guard's van of a passenger train just helped to produce greater earnings from the same outlay. Based on this reasoning railways in the peak years of this century carried every conceivable small and special consignment for every type of private and commercial purpose and only since nationalisation has the freight sundries business been disposed of and parcels movement by passenger train cut back to station to station conveyance only.

The reasons are understandable, for the handling of small consignments is a very labour intensive business and can only be efficient and profitable if the maximum use is made of mechanised sorting to expedite handling, reduce its costs and concentrate traffic for one destination into full load quantities. The big railway companies did all this so that at the end of the Great Western Railway era

Interior of a goods sundries depot, with parcels being sorted on a conveyor belt

depots like the one at Bristol Temple Meads had become show pieces of traffic handling. A great many systems were tried — conveyor belts, wagon loading and unloading machines and even 'slave' trolleys — and they all helped. Small wheeled (SW) containers were offered to fill the gap between the collapsible Collico containers and the 1 ton 'A' container, but the service never really got away from its old fashioned and costly methods.

Looked at in retrospect the movement process for a small consignment by goods train seems horrifying. If it originated in a country area and required collection a 'Call Order', passed from the goods clerk taking the sender's request to the motor driver of the appropriate cartage round, would ensure that a railway vehicle picked up the package on the day when it was next scheduled to serve that particular area. Unless the sender had a credit account it would then not get forwarded until he had visited the goods office, made out a consignment note and paid the appropriate sum. Since the station was too small to load more than one van of these mixed consignments daily, the best the sender could expect would be that his goods would be safely placed in the van being loaded in the goods shed for attaching to the daily service, which arrived from some nearby larger yard or depot with incoming traffic or empties and cleared the wagons loaded in the yard or shed. At some places the consignment might not pass through the goods shed but be placed straight in the 'road van' of the local pick-up train, but in both cases the consignment would be weighed and the consignment note passed to the office for an invoice to be completed as the basis both for the accounting and for advising the destination that the goods were on their way.

The van in which the small consignments were loaded would now be on its way to some larger centre. From the train arrival point it would be moved by a pilot engine to the goods transhipment depot's reception line and finally positioned for unloading in the shed by the pilot, by gravity, by horse or capstan shunting, by a truck moving machine, or even by some hard pushing by the shed staff. Once

Temple Meads goods depot, Bristol and its local signal box

inside the shed, the van's contents would be unloaded to be resorted with the goods being forwarded on the depot's own account, a process involving a great deal of lifting and carrying as dozens of goods porters wheeled their hand barrows across the raised wooden platforms from one wagon to another or from the tailboard of a cartage vehicle to the weighing machine. If the transit was an easy one the consignment would now travel in a through wagon to its destination, although it still had to survive the shocks of intermediate marshalling and the eagle eyes of the Carriage and Wagon staff whose job was to examine freight trains at given intervals and have shunted out any wagons with hot axle boxes or other defects.

At last the consignment arrives at the destination depot, again shunted from yard to shed but now ready for unloading. Thanks to the skills of the staff at the forwarding end no larger or heavier parcel has rolled on it, no threatening liquid has been loaded in an unsuitable receptacle and the choice of a weather-tight van has kept the rain at bay during the journey. From the invoice the consignment has been listed on a delivery sheet and the unloaded goods are checked against this before being wheeled to one of the many bays used for loading to the cartage vehicles. As mechanical horses took over from rigid vehicles the use of articulated trailers allowed spare trailers to be loaded at any time so that a full load was ready and waiting for the tractor when it returned from its previous round. So, at last, our consignment gets delivered but it has been a long and complicated process and the package has spent more time waiting and being handled than it has moving towards its destination.

Generally speaking the movement of small items by passenger train tended to be simpler, although life could be very hectic at a big parcels depot and there could be some hair-raising movements as barrow loads of parcels were pushed across the sleeper crossings of many main line stations with very little margin before an express thundered through. The variety of traffic sent by the parcels service was at least as great as that going by goods although its nature was different, samples instead of bags of manure, live fish instead of bags of nails and silks instead of drums of lubricating oil. The railways publicised their parcels facilities and rates more openly for their customers were as much the ordinary family wanting to move an item too large to go by post as the world of business.

A look at the provisions made by the railways for the conveyance of parcels provides an interesting view of the activities of an age. In the era before World War I considerable use was made of agents for the receipt of parcels and these included tramway companies, 'Draper and Gent's Mercers', 'Livery and Bait Stables', as well as chemists, tobacconists, printers and newsagents. Traffic specially provided for included:

Articles Frail or very Bulky in Proportion to Weight — such as cases of stuffed birds, common clay pipes, wax figures, phonograph cylinders, mantles for incandescent gas lights, saccharometers and symphoniums — were all conveyed at the owner's risk and subject to the payment of a supplement to the ordinary parcels rate.

Railway Letter Post — by paying 2d for 'A Special Railway Adhesive Label', letters already bearing the ordinary 1d stamp would be conveyed by train, either to await collection at destination or to be posted there. If the sender liked to telegraph the 'Postmaster of the nearest Postal Telegraph Office to the station of arrival' he could have a special messenger to collect the letter from the train and complete its delivery.

Newspapers — quite separate from the bulk movement of newspapers was a facility for sending small numbers to cater for remote subscribers of newspapers, periodicals and other printed works. The senders could buy stamps which they affixed to cover the cost of the package being despatched, but the railway warned them, 'In the case of Two or more Newspapers folded together being insufficiently stamped the Packet will be detained for one train, and charged double the amount of deficiency, as is done with letters by Post.'

Envelopes containing 'News Intelligence' were also conveyed, also grain samples and, in the case of the Great Central 'Baskets of Linen to or from the Laundry at Grimsby'. The London, Brighton and South Coast Railway was ready to convey empties, including fish empties, boats and canoes, milk in churns, and three delightful mixed categories which take some beating for variety, viz:

Muffins, Bacon, Biscuits, Bread, Cakes (except Bride Cakes), Yeast, Pork Pies, Sausages, Baskets containing Laundry, Plants and Flowers.

Bicycles, Tricycles, Sociables (the Liberty Sociable was an attachment for motor cycles, a side carrier similar to a trailer), Hawkers' Hand Carts, Two-Wheeled Hand Carts containing Electric Testing Machinery (for what, one wonders), Scissor Grinders' Machines, Street Pianos and Ice Cream Carts.

Consignments of an Exceptional Nature, viz Barrel Organ; Harp, Bass Viol, Double Bass or Violincello; Bulls; Cartridges; Cats; Coffins; Cow and Calf; Small Birds; Manual and Steam Fire Engines; Mare accompanied by a Foal; Oxen and Cow; Pianofortes or Harmoniums; Pony or a Donkey.

Certain types of luggage passed so regularly and in such quantities as to constitute a significant parcels traffic activity. The free allowance went up to 3cwt for first class travellers and 1½cwt for third class passengers if they were commercial travellers, members of theatrical companies, music hall artistes,

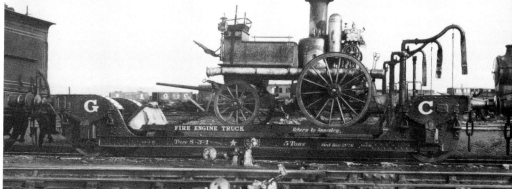

A horse drawn steam fire engine sits on a Great Central Railway well wagon by courtesy of a special Fire Engine Truck platform

Increased free luggage weight allowances were given to commercial travellers and other special groups, eg:

Professional Swimmers engaged at Music Halls to give Exhibitions of Swimming in Tanks fixed upon the Stage

The following will be treated and charged in the same way as Commercial Travellers' Luggage at Owners' risk, and at Ordinary Excess Luggage Rates at Companys's risk:-

Demonstration Plant used by Lecturers employed by County Councils, Technical Schools, &c., including Schools of Cookery.

Demonstration Plant of Lecturers employed by the Church of England Incorporated Society for providing homes for Waifs and Strays.

Demonstration Plant of Lady Lecturers connected with Gas Engineers and Cooking Stove Manufacturers.

Dissolving View and other apparatus accompanying Band of Hope Lecturers who travel in various parts of the country.

Lecturing Apparatus of the Secretary of the National Refuge for Homeless and Destitute Children, when accompanied by the Secretary of the Institution.

Luggage of Lecturers for the Society for the Propagation of the Gospel in Foreign Parts.

Luggage accompanying Deputation Secretaries lecturing on behalf of the National Incorporated Association for the Reclamation of Destitute Waif Children, otherwise known as Dr Barnardo's Homes.

Luggage belonging to Deputation Secretaries and Lecturers of the Church Army.

Emigrants' Luggage from Hull, New Holland, Grimsby, and Grimsby Docks to Liverpool:- 1s per cwt. From Liverpool to Hull, New Holland, Grimsby, and Grimsby Docks, 2s 4d per cwt. No excess charge to be made unless amounting to 1s or upwards.

Many movements required the provision of special vehicles and/or special treatment. Examples include theatrical scenery which had to be moved to a tight schedule which would allow its dismantling, movement and re-erection in the intervals between the end of the Saturday night performance and the beginning of the week's engagement in another town which could be miles away. Many such special trains were run and some flows were catered for by regular trains, put on for theatrical traffic but available to ordinary passengers as well. An example of the latter was the Sunday service between Cardiff and Sheffield which commenced on 8 April 1906. Routed via Banbury, one leg left Sheffield at 9.50am and the northbound working left Cardiff at 12.25pm. At the end of the 1920s a 9.10am was put on from Bristol to Paddington and nicely filled a gap in the ordinary service which would otherwise have had no train between 4.05am and 12.30pm. A return service at 7.30pm filled the gap between 5.30pm and 9.50pm.

members of equestrian parties or professional swimmers. Among the items which commercial travellers were not allowed to treat as luggage but were charged, instead, special rates were patent corking machines, automatic 'Penny-in-the-Slot' pianos, sausage making machines, small gas engines and patent scrubbing machines. Not so well favoured were 'workpeople taking with them at their own risk, either to or from warehouses or manufactories, work which they do at their own homes' and 'Hucksters, Travelling Drapers, or Packmen' who only got a free weight allowance of 60lb.

Most of the railway livestock movements by passenger train were 'one-off' workings in fitted horse boxes or cattle trucks attached to the rear of an existing service. The range of facilities offered was again considerable. At one end of the scale, both socially and in rate terms, came officers' horses, hunting horses and polo ponies and at the other livestock movements for dealers who received a discount of 20 per cent on the 'Ordinary Horse Rate' for sending twelve or more animals together. The requirements of the racing seasons were another comprehensive and colourful activity with the special trains for passengers on race days being preceded and followed by the movement of the race horses themselves. Facilities were also provided for brood mares and stallions travelling for breeding purposes and high class livestock was regularly conveyed to and from agricultural shows. 'Hounds in Hound Vans' were charged at the same rate as two horses, but two ponies not exceeding twelve hands cost only as much as a horse and a half! Mules, goats, cattle, sheep and pigs usually went by goods train but pets or especially valuable animals might ride in the guard's van along with muzzled dogs or calves in sacks if their owners would pay the higher costs involved.

In the years at the beginning of the century private carriages and the early motor car models existed side by side and the railways happily carried either on flat carriage trucks. Potential sellers might send such items for sale at an agricultural show or on approval, or might forward them for loan or repair and be charged only half rate when they came back. It was possible to send by rail a hearse, with or without corpse, a showman's van for repair or even an organ but 'Furniture Vans, Tramway Cars and Engines of Steam Roundabouts' were not accepted by passenger train. Some movements were highly individual, others involved private vans like those conveying works of art loaned for exhibition by the South Kensington Museum or the instruments of the Scottish Orchestra Company. Yet other carriage truck movements eventually took a public form like the service provided by the Great Western for conveying motor cars through the Severn Tunnel from Pilning to Severn Tunnel Junction to save drivers the long journey up the estuary to Gloucester and down the other side or a possible rough trip across the ferry.

Mail and newspapers by passenger train are still important to the railway system after many years in which virtually the whole distribution activity lay in their hands. At night the large stations become the scene of hundreds of scurrying post office trolleys, with vans of newspapers adding to the bustle as the first editions roll off the presses.

Mail traffic transferred from road to rail early in the railway era, the Liverpool and Manchester Railway carrying letters by two services daily within weeks of

Mail exchange apparatus

opening and the transfer process accelerating as the linking of towns by railway widened. The effect on business activity was considerable since, in most cases, a day was saved in the communication and action cycle. The facilities for letters were eventually followed by the development of the parcels post which supplemented the railways' own parcels business, the two together allowing the development of a massive mail order activity.

The railways were obliged to carry mail by statute but, in turn, derived a useful contractual revenue and the two organisations produced a number of special facilities from their liaison. One example was the TPO (Travelling Post Office) vehicle — still in use — on which letter sorting takes place while the train is in motion. One of the many curious sideline facilities of the railway network was that of posting letters in a special letter box provided in the side panels of TPO vehicles. Sorting en route also takes place in newspaper vans but that other railway phenomenon, lineside apparatus for catching bags of mail from trains travelling at speed and for delivering bags to them, can now only be seen in a preservation setting at places like the Didcot Railway Centre.

In addition to its major contracts for the carriage of mail and newspapers the railways were prepared to arrange Agreed Flat Rates for the regular, system-wide movement of smalls traffic, both parcels and goods sundries, for commercial firms. These Agreed Flat Rates involved a commuted per package charge irrespective of weight or destination, the figure being arrived at by an initial test with ordinary charges with subsequent short-period tests being used to modify the charge and reflect changes in the product, its traffic pattern or the railways' own level of rates. Thousands of items, as diverse as toilet seats or hampers of game and poultry, were distributed daily under this system.

Railways showed themselves just as willing to handle occasional and unusual traffic as they were to move regular forwardings, although the financial rewards could rarely have covered the true costs involved. In the age of the great travelling circuses moves of any distance were arranged with the help of the railway company's special traffic canvasser. Well before the last performance was given in the big top the flat wagons, horse boxes, cattle trucks and covered vans needed for the move would be moving into the local station. The expertise of the circus erection and dismantling staff would be matched by that of the railwaymen as poles and canvas were craned onto wagons and secured, horses coaxed into horse boxes and their hay and water supplies placed in with them, and the performers made sure that their luggage and props were safely stowed in the luggage van. The caged animals were usually no problem but coaxing a small elephant into a covered carriage truck could be exhausting for the handlers and hilarious for the onlookers, especially when the confused animal felt obliged to relieve himself in the middle of the pushing, shoving and cajoling process.

In addition to works and farm removals one other railway speciality, even more complex, was the servicing of major agricultural shows, so much a part of the English country scene. Exhibitors came from all over the country and might bring anything from large agricultural machines to outsize display panels. The vast animal contingent would be equally varied and to find vehicles, plan train services, lay on reception and unloading accommodation and provide vehicles for delivery to the site called for a great deal of skill from the sales and traffic staff of the railway. The seasoned cartage inspector in charge of the delivery arrangements would be wise enough to get plenty of ropes and sleepers up to the showground so that he could tackle the awkward unloading job and avoid the embarrassment of his mobile crane sinking into the mud, but he might still find that an energetic canvasser had done his job so well that the equipment that had brought everything in on time was inadequate for all the business to be moved away once the show was over.

Behind all these activities, routine or spectacular, was the vast railway network and its administrative organisation sometimes doing its job as a matter of course, at others performing highly enterprising and spectacular feats.

THE RAILWAY AT WORK 11

With railways involved so deeply in the affairs of everyday life it was inevitable that they should build up a sizeable operational and administrative activity relatively little of which was apparent to the casual observer. He saw only lines, trains and stations yet the railways employed hundreds of thousands of staff at countless different locations and required of them a vast variety of skills. They had not only to drive trains, plan services and operate them safely, but also to maintain machinery and equipment, account for monies and deal with such diverse subjects as local rating, siting of signals, gas fitting, advertising or preparing a new Parliamentary Bill.

At the modest sized station there might be just one clerk on duty at most times and he would have to handle the whole range of the passenger train activities. The booking part was relatively easy and it was possible to issue tickets very rapidly unless someone wanted to travel to a destination for which no printed stock was held when the fare had to be calculated, a blank card made out and its issue recorded in a separate register. Some tickets might be cut diagonally, or have a portion removed, eg to convert an adult issue to that of a child. This cut down the range of tickets which had to be held — perhaps single, return, child, workmens, excursion and cheap day for each significant destination — but meant careful storage of the ticket portion remaining to justify the lower sum put into the till. Also difficult in terms of holding up the queue for tickets were warrants which had to be exchanged for paper tickets, a party heading for some central event and producing an identity card to demonstrate entitlement to the party rate or a fellow railwayman taking advantage of his concessionary fare entitlement and needing the completion of a blank 'privilege' ticket and the calculation of the amount of his quarter fare.

The booking clerk at such a station might also have to look after the parcels counter and in addition to booking trains, answering enquiries and dealing with cloakroom deposits or withdrawals, also accept consignments brought in by the public or the carmen. Each must be weighed and charged out, a consignment note had to be completed covering the details of the transaction and embodying the conditions under which it was carried and the package itself needed stamps to the value of the amount paid or the affixing of a ledger label if the sender had a credit account. The parcels stamps were of various monetary values and needed to be balanced with the money taken. Seven varieties of ledger label covered various permutations of service, some traders only requiring station to station conveyance, others collection and delivery within ordinary limits and yet others

LONDON TILBURY & SOUTHEND RAILWAY.

C.O. 1054.

FENCHURCH STREET TERMINUS,
December 9th, 1897.

HOURS of DUTY AND PAY of SIGNALMEN.

On and after SATURDAY, 11th instant, all former Regulations as to Time, Pay and Allowances, will be cancelled, and the following will come into operation :

Wages will be calculated at Six days per week, and when overtime has to be made or duty undertaken Seven days in a week, the Seventh day shall be paid for at the same rate per day.

No Signalman who may be required to work part of the Seventh day will be paid less than for a quarter of a day.

The Scale of Pay per Week will be as follows :

	1st YEAR.	2nd YEAR.	3rd YEAR.	4th YEAR.
1st Class	23/-	24/-	25/-	26/-
2nd ,,	22/-	23/-	24/-	25/-
3rd ,,	21/-	22/-	23/-	24/-
4th ,,	20/-	21/-	22/-	23/-

An allowance of 3/- per week to be allowed to all Signalmen in the London District up to and including Barking East Junction Signal-box in all cases where the Company does not provide Cottages at a rent not exceeding 4/- per week, and this allowance to be made until the Company is prepared to offer the Signalmen cottages at a rent not exceeding 4/- per week.

Porter Signalmen to be classed from this date as fourth-rate Signalmen.

Six days holiday (to be taken before July or after September) with pay and passes to any place on the Company's Line will be allowed once a year.

CLASSIFICATION OF BOXES AND HOURS OF DUTY.

FIRST CLASS.	Hours of Duty	SECOND CLASS.	Hours of Duty	THIRD CLASS.	Hours of Duty	FOURTH CLASS.	Hours of Duty
Bromley ...	8	East Ham ...	10	Upton Park ...	10	Dagenham ...	12
Abbey Mills Junc.	8	East Ham Loop Junc.	10	Rippleside ...	10	Hornchurch ...	12
Plaistow ...	8	Woodgrange Park ...	10	Upminster ...	10	Romford ...	12
		Barking West Junc.	10	Upminster East Junc.	10	East Horndon ...	12
		Tanner Street ...	8	Rainham ...	10	Laindon ...	12
		Barking Station ...	8	Ordnance Crossing ...	10	Ockendon ...	12
		Barking East Junc.	8	Purfleet ...	10	West Thurrock Siding	12
		Tilbury West Junc.	10	West Thurrock Junc.	10	Low Street ...	12
		Tilbury South Junc.	10	Grays... ...	10	Thames Haven Junc.	12
				Tilbury North Junc.	10	Stanford-le-Hope	12
				Tilbury Docks ...	10	Benfleet ...	12
				Tilbury East Junc.	10	Westcliff ...	12
				Pitsea Junction ...	10		
				Leigh... ...	10		
				Southend ...	10		
				Southend East	10		
				Shoeburyness	10		

A Copy of this order to be handed to each Signalman.

Each Station Master to please acknowledge the receipt of the proper number of orders supplied to the Signalmen appointed in his district and arrange accordingly.

B. BULLOCK,
Assistant Manager.

*Hours and pay for signalmen on the London
Tilbury and Southend line*

the debiting back of any extra delivery or other charges which might be incurred in completing the transaction. Arriving from the trains were more consignments, anything from a box of fish to a muzzled dog or the mast for a sailing dinghy. No sooner were these entered on the carman's delivery sheet or the counter sheet than the day's despatches of cut flowers might start arriving or the local pigeon fanciers turn up with the hampers of birds which the railways undertook to despatch and then release at a specific time and place.

Travel enquiries were a regular occurrence in the booking clerk's day and he would know off by heart the times of the local trains and the connections they made, but for longer journeys the task was more difficult. After grouping the exchange of timetables between companies became general but there were frequently several routes by which a journey might be made and the policy behind each company's fares and ticket availability remained to secure the maximum portion of the journey to its own route so that in the division of receipts effected by the Railway Clearing House it might retain as much of the fare paid by the traveller as possible.

On top of these major activities the booking clerk had many other duties. For many years ticket collection was undertaken by special staff either on the train or at special ticket platforms, but as the closed station concept spread — on the Great Western in the years just before World War I — the collection of tickets at stations too small to have their own ticket collectors devolved upon porters or booking office staff. This brought them all sorts of complications, one of the greatest deriving from attempts to prevent cheap fares, offered where they could stimulate more travel, from being used between places where they were invalid. A typical example, albeit from 1905, was a cheap fare facility from Manchester to Yarmouth which was used by a passenger who alighted at Brundall. There he was told that his ticket was not valid and that he could either pay the difference between the fare he had already paid and the ordinary fare to Brundall or go on to Yarmouth and return from there. He did the latter but subsequently wrote to the press:

> '. . . It [the Great Eastern Railway] cannot possibly contend that it is more profitable to convey a passenger the 24 miles to Yarmouth and back for payment than to accept the same payment without performing the service. . . . Such corporations can be compared with those who raise themselves to opulence from small beginnings and retain a pettifogging and disputatious spirit.'

This attack brought a stinging reply, signed by 'Claud J. Hamilton' himself. He maintained that the gentleman from Manchester should have known when he entered into the contract that the ticket was for Yarmouth only and by alighting at Brundall he was depriving the railway of 6s 8½d. The Chairman of the Great Eastern Railway cordially invited to Yarmouth 'all other Manchester men who are prepared to make a proper use of our cheap week-end tickets.'

Along with the closed station concept came the introduction of platform tickets. In the Bristol district of the Great Western Railway Chippenham became the first station to issue the new 1d tickets in 1912 and in the following year Bath was provided with an automatic machine which cost £40. One of the booking clerk's jobs was to keep these machines filled with tickets and to empty the pennies and account for them. In later years he was to perform the same service for the companies supplying the chocolate and other machines, while a small source of additional income was the twopence in the shilling commission he received from selling travel insurance.

The work of other parts of the station was as varied as that in the booking office.

Typical railway signal box, in this case watching over the celebrated Llandudno-Manchester Club Train

In the goods yard a yard inspector might control both the full load work in the main yard and the goods sundries handling through the shed. He would have a foreman to supervise each of these aspects, the one in the yard being a working foreman and expected to deal with the shunting in conjunction with the train guards. All stations of any size had a weighbridge where the load to be charged for was established by deducting the tare weight of the cart or lorry from the total weight and where public weighing was undertaken for a fee. Frequently the weighbridgeman might also make out the wagon labels but with a roaring fire in the range and the teapot handy in one of the brown painted cupboards it was no bad place to be, especially in the winter when other staff might be wrestling with a stiff, damp tarpaulin or trying to control a container being lifted by the yard crane in a stiff wind.

There was usually a good fire in the porters' room as well, but none was permitted in the lamp room where all the hand lamps, platform lamps and signal lamps were looked after. Fresh oil or paraffin was needed regularly, wicks had to be cleaned or replaced and lamp glasses had to be kept well polished. After going the rounds of the platforms, crossing gates, station buildings and yard lamps there was then the task of climbing the signal posts to change the lamps there. The compensation was a visit to the signal box to check that the signalman was satisfied that he could see the back lights at night, there being few boxes that failed to keep a good fire and ready tea. Not that anyone begrudged the signalman these comforts for the bells, levers, train register book and single needle telegraph kept him pretty busy and pulling off a distant signal, with a mile of wire between the lever and the arm itself, was no easy matter.

There were few sinecures in the railway industry. The footplate world might appear glamorous but it was a long climb from cleaner to 'passed fireman', through the firing links and then from shunting driver up to the top link on the main line. Many an oily rag would be worn out, many a ton of coal shovelled and many a dirty, clinker-clogged fire coaxed back to life on the way. Having to drop fires or put away engines after a long firing trip on a bad steamer was hard, unpleasant work and many locomotives, especially those with driving wheels under the cab or just back from shops, were highly uncomfortable to ride on. Add the discomforts of tender first running on a wet winter day and it becomes surprising that becoming an engine driver was such a universal ambition.

In the locomotive world, as in that of goods yards and passenger stations, a great many people were at work behind the scenes. Long before a train's driver and fireman booked on the steam raiser would have been called by the knocker-up tapping on his window, walked or cycled to the depot and started lighting up in the fireboxes of the first engines booked out. He used firelighters made of pieces of sawn sleeper crossed two on two and filled in with shed waste and oily rag, lighting these and building up small coal on top until the fire had taken hold. The fireman, booked on duty well in advance of the time the engine was due to leave shed, would then take over and coax the fire up to full steam pressure. As he did so the driver would arrive, having read all the notices about speed restrictions or engineering work on his route and perhaps talked to the running shed foreman about some detail of the diagrams and rosters posted on the huge notice boards. The coalman having loaded the tender, by hand or beneath one of the huge concrete silos into which wagons of coal were raised and tipped, the engine could take water and then head for the local yard or station and the train it was to work. Others contributing to the process included the sand furnace attendants who cared for the furnace in which sand for use in the locomotive sanding gear was dried, the shed turners who moved engines about the shed, fire droppers and ash loaders, and a whole host of fitting and maintenance staff. Supervising the whole activity was a shed master who might be involved in commenting on a draft timetable one day and the next getting into a firebox to inspect a brick arch or supervising the rerailing of a locomotive which had 'come off the road'.

Each of the many faces of the railway activity had its fascination and influence. Each was a miniature empire with a functional officer at the head and reporting to the general manager, and each had its own local officers — District Passenger Superintendents, District Engineers, District Motive Power Superintendents, District Outdoor Machinery Engineers, District Signal and Telegraph Engineers, District Goods Superintendents and the like. But no department wielded more power or had more influence on the way the railway affected the lives of its users than the traffic or operating department. The District Operating Superintendent was the one who carried the timetable into practice and provided for all the planned and unplanned situations that this involved. His staff manned the signal boxes, worked the stations and yards, controlled and implemented the movement regulations and catered for countless additional capacity requirements, from the provision of relief crossing keepers to organising the movements of the royal train.

In addition to its many routine tasks, the operating department was very involved in special traffic movements like the conveyance of hop pickers from London to the Kent hop fields. Each year whole families spent August and September picking the crop during the day, providing their own special brand of entertainment in the evening and sleeping in huts or tents adjacent to the hop fields. Father might have to stay at his regular job but he pushed the barrow from the Elephant and Castle area to London Bridge as the rest of the family, laden with bags, mattresses and cooking utensils, set out for the annual exodus. Each weekend at the beginning of the season up to half a dozen trains would depart between 3am and 6am, made up of ancient stock dragged out of semi-retirement at Maze Hill and Blackheath, and heading for Maidstone, Paddock Wood or the Hawkhurst branch.

Special hop pickers' period tickets were available for those spending the whole of the August and September season down in Kent and more special trains and fares were available each weekend for 'hop pickers' friends' or for fathers joining the picking activity for the one week they could get off work. These Sunday trains were stabled at Hawkhurst until the evening and then worked back again for use the next weekend or for the end of season return to 'The Smoke'. The whole affair was a lively one with children hidden under the masses of luggage to dodge the travelling ticket collectors and so much pulling of the communication cord that the only way to get the train home was to disconnect the vacuum and work on the engine brake alone.

The operating department's control office operated round the clock to deal with abnormal situations. It not only took the minute by minute decisions about whether or not to hold a connection for a late running train or finding a substitute for a driver or guard who had not reported for duty, but also acted as the centre for traffic regulation in emergencies. The concept of centralised train control had originated with the Midland Railway which had developed a scheme for supervising movements in the dense industrial area around Sheffield, Derby and Nottingham out of an experiment originally designed to reduce the long hours of train crews. The Midland Railway went on to develop district control centres covering the whole of its freight traffic working, with a headquarters central control to co-ordinate the activity and another central control for passenger train operations. The London and North Western appointed district controllers responsible through district superintendents and the Lancashire and Yorkshire provided a control centre at Manchester with sub-controls at outlying points to deal with local workings. After grouping the London, Midland and Scottish built upon this start and was the first of the big four railways to provide a control organisation embracing virtually the whole of its system.

Until the development of an express freight train pattern in the early years of the century the movement of goods was a much less disciplined activity than that applying to passenger trains. The normal practice was for the station master or yard master at the originating point to despatch trains when it suited their own working arrangements and for them to then stagger on from district to district, depending almost entirely on local convenience and irrespective of the overall situation. As traffic levels increased and fast and efficient movement became more important this approach had to go, World War I further underlining its inadequacies and wastage and the advent of the eight-hour day for enginemen

Royal Trains

Royalty has always made full use of railways, even from the earliest days, and their special coaches were headed by immaculately prepared locomotives

Notice covering the journey of HM Queen Mary from Edinburgh to Harrogate on 12 September 1938

MONDAY, 12th SEPTEMBER.

Time Table for Train

convèying

HER MAJESTY QUEEN MARY

From Edinburgh to Harrogate

Her Majesty Queen Mary and Suite will travel from Edinburgh (Waverley) at 11.20 a.m. to Harrogate by the Pullman Car train leaving Edinburgh (Waverley) at 11.20 a.m. (Glasgow (Queen Street) 10.15 a.m.) which is timed to run from Edinburgh as follows :—

STATIONS	TIME		
	ARRIVE	PASS	DEPART
	A.M.	A.M.	A.M.
			11 20
		11 26	
		11 30	
EDINBURGH WAVERLEY (10 platform)		11 37½	11 43
PORTOBELLO			
MONKTONHALL JUNCTION	11 42		
LONGNIDDRY JUNCTION		11 55½	
DREM JUNCTION		12 11½	
DUNBAR		12 16	
GRANTSHOUSE		12 25	
RESTON JUNCTION		12 27	
MARSHALL MEADOWS		12 42½	
BERWICK		12 59	
BELFORD		1 18½	1 45
ALNMOUTH	1 41		
MORPETH		1 48	
NEWCASTLE (No. 10 platform)		1 54	
KING EDWARD BRIDGE		2 5½	
BIRTLEY		2 19½	2 34
DURHAM			
FERRYHILL	2 33	2 41	
DARLINGTON		2 50	
ERYHOLME		3 4	
NORTHALLERTON			
RIPON	3 20		
HARROGATE (No. 5 platform)			

The Trains will be fitted with and controlled by the vacuum brake.

FORMATION OF TRAIN LEAVING EDINBURGH (WAVERLEY) :—

Brake Third No. 1516 (Brake end leading).

Her Majesty'ır Saloon No. 395 (Attendant's balcony end leading).

Brake First No. 4188 (Brake end trailing).

7 Pullman cars.

WORKING NOTES :—

Pacific type locomotive fitted with corridor tender to be provided to work train from Edinburgh to Harrogate and Leeds.

HARROGATE :—

The Train will arrive at No. 5 platform and must come to a stand with the cab of the engine opposite a point at which a flagman will be standing exhibiting a red flag.

The Special portion (3 empty vehicles) will work through to Leeds Central, be detached there from the Pullman train and sent to Doncaster Shops for stabling by the 5.55 p.m. O.P. (**464/2**).

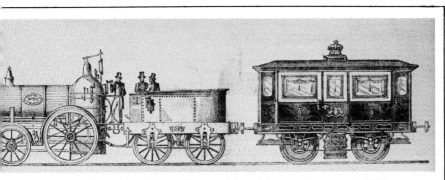

The London and Birmingham Railway's Bury *2-2-0 No 20 plus royal carriage in 1843*

The London and North Western royal train headed by 4082 Windsor Castle *proudly bearing the royal train headlamps*

finally ensuring its demise. By the time the next war overtook the railways the control system had been developed to a fine art, especially on the London and North Eastern Railway where almost every traffic point on the system was linked by telephone to the control network.

The control system more than proved its worth during World War II, moving every type of passenger from evacuees to troops heading for the Normandy beachheads and every type of freight from bullets to Bailey bridges. The communication and organisational skills which had been so sharpened in the process remained available for the peacetime railway. They were put to use, in fact, as early as 1946-7 when a hard winter brought heavy snow in Norfolk and the adjacent Fen lands. The snowploughs were ordered out but could not keep the lines open. One by one they closed, trapping trains and passengers and needing the rescue operations mounted through the control network to free them. The controllers organised labour to dig out the stranded — including negotiations for the use of some Italian prisoners of war who had not then been repatriated — and then turned their attention to planning and introducing an emergency train service.

No sooner had the tired railwaymen of all grades finished the task of rescuing passengers and trains, clearing the lines and getting the locomotives and rolling stock back onto their normal workings than the thaw set it and soon the many rivers and streams of the flat, fertile area were bulging with the extra water. Unable to contain it for long, the rivers burst their banks and the water poured out over acres of farmland and miles of railway line. In the control office the reports of lonely signal boxes and crossings were gathered together and senior traffic officers were in constant touch with their civil engineering colleagues

Rerailing derailed vehicles could often be done with ramps and packing but this one was a heavy lift job for the breakdown cranes

Accidents will happen! This one outside the bonded tobacco store at Bristol

whose permanent way was under more and more pressure from the weight of moving water. Services were rerouted and reorganised until the water finally took command and flooded all the routes out of Norfolk, except the Midland and Great Northern line via Melton Constable and King's Lynn. Even when the floods began to subside pilot engines had to be turned out to test each stretch of track and a service planned to capitalise on whatever routes could be used without repacking of the ballast or clearing trees and other debris. Eventually all lines and services returned to normal but the backlog of freight and parcels still had to be cleared and the control office would play a major part in this as it had in the dramas of the preceding days.

In ideal circumstances the railway traffic would move without reference to the control organisation. Trains were planned to work to pre-determined running times, line occupation was graphed so that each service had a 'path' which would avoid it delaying or being delayed by other trains and locomotive, carriage and train crews' diagrams were designed to provide men and equipment to operate all services. Each station or depot was equipped to receive and despatch trains to time and put in a lot of local effort to see that this was done.

At a seaside terminus, like Clacton-on-Sea, the weekday working normally produced few problems and could be left to the station inspectors and their platform staff. But summer Saturdays were a different matter for the platforms and circulating area capacity remained the same and there was only one engine turntable, but the number of trains doubled and the number of passengers ran into tens of thousands. The local plan detailed each arrival and showed the next working of the footplatemen, the locomotive, the carriage set and the guard. It indicated whether the train was to be stopped short of the end of its arrival platform so that the engine could be released or whether it should come right in and be loaded and re-engined immediately. Staffing was arranged to cope with the expected levels of traffic, some idea of which could be gained from the previous year's experience and from discussions with the local holiday camps to establish their level of bookings. Well before the first holidaymakers had gone to bed on the Friday night, Clacton was ready for its weekly Saturday inundation.

If things went well the situation was just a question of hard work and perseverance for the railway staff but on some occasions all their professional skills would be needed to move the vast numbers who needed the trains to provide their holiday travel. On a really bad day one of the early trains might be late arriving so that its guard and locomotive might not be available for the departure they should have worked. If the delay was known early enough it might be possible to find another guard or locomotive intended to work to the same destination at a later time and simply change the two arrangements over. If this easy solution was not available it was only possible to take any guard who was willing to work the job, any locomotive with a suitable route availability and any enginemen who 'knew the road' and hope to fill the gaps that using them would create. On such days the station master used all his ingenuity to keep trains moving, getting the help and agreement of the control office where he could, but sometimes having to make the decision and then ask the control to make good its effects on other destinations and connections.

All it needed to upset the intricate balance of such situations, not untypical in terms of the service provided by the railways over many years, was an engine of the wrong type to work in, a guard asked to work an arrival to solve someone else's emergency, to have run out of hours or need a food break, or a coach to become derailed while being set back from the running lines into the carriage sidings. By the time the breakdown van could be got to the latter hundreds of passengers could have been seriously inconvenienced and the station master had to decide whether the derailed vehicle could be put back by using one of the train engines, his local ramps and bits of sleepers as packing. If the makeshift arrangement worked it was just part of what was expected from the local railwaymen, if it did not the situation might be made worse and have to await the arrival of the breakdown van from Colchester or even the crane from Stratford.

Many of these complications eased as railways were modernised — and enginemen at Clacton merely walked from one end of an arriving electrical multiple unit to the other to make it a train ready for departure — but for many, many years they were part of the working service to the community.

From the middle of the last century to the middle of this one there can have been few lives and activities not touched by the railways in one way or another. The effect was not always that resulting from the conveyance of passengers and goods but could arise from factors as diverse as the use of the railways' ten o'clock telegraph time signal to supplant local timekeeping or their huge purchasing power as consumers of coal, steel and many other commodities. Railways also affected the fabric of the nation by their status as employers. By 1900 the system was employing over 400,000 people directly and securing the jobs of the thousands more engaged in providing supplies or services for the railway activity.

By 1900 the character of the railway workforce had changed from the cosmopolitan mixture of the early years. Initially taking in large numbers with poor selection procedures and little organised training had given the early companies a high turnover and constant problems from staff rudeness, lateness, absenteeism and drunkenness. However, the value of an interesting and steady job coupled with a rigid system of discipline, a strict and understandable hierarchy and a substantial degree of paternalism provided stability for many years. The first trade union to emerge was the Railway Clerks' Association — now the Transport Salaried Staffs Association. This was in 1865, two years before the bitter battle in which the North Eastern Railway fought and beat a strike by the Engine Drivers and Firemens' Society. Despite this outcome the 1867 strike helped to create a process of negotiation and staff improvements that helped the railways through some difficult years. It led to better wages and conditions, bringing the first real recognition that long hours were anti-social and a prime cause of accidents and keeping the possibility of a national railway strike at bay for another 44 years. The age of the damaging strike began in 1920-2 and a rail strike followed the General Strike in 1926, resulting in a few lines being closed permanently and some business being lost to the plentiful supply of road hauliers. But the elements of interest, discipline, hierarchy and paternalism were still stabilising factors and kept thousands in secure, well-paid employment in which the overwhelming majority took great pride.

Great Western Railway staff registers of the 1870s show its station masters as receiving anything from £80 a year (at Savernake) to £199 a year (at Bristol). The Bristol station master was 53 and his senior booking clerk 62, but the chief clerk in the superintendent's office was only 40 and already earned £200 annually. Lad

Clerk Smith had to manage on £20 a year when he started work at Bath on 28 August 1876 but when Mr Howell, the station master there, retired on reaching the age of 64 he was receiving the grand sum of £300 per annum. Howell had been twenty-five when he started his career with the infant Great Western Railway and had been looking after the company's interests at Bath for almost twenty years. These registers throw a lot of light on railway employment as a career and their remarks columns carry such revealing comments as 'Pensioned by the Board', 'Passed Senior Clerks Examination', 'Resigned to better self' and 'Would not do'.

A notable feature of the railway community scene was the railway towns. In the case of Crewe there were less than 300 people in the area when the Grand Junction Railway opened a station there in 1837 but from the opening of the locomotive works on 2 September 1843 the settlement expanded rapidly. Workmens' cottages, public baths, schools, and even doctors and clergy, were provided by the railway, the church itself being completed with the dividends of those directors who declined to profit from the running of Sunday trains. At first purely a railway community, elected local residents were gradually admitted to the governing body until Crewe Local Board was formed in 1877. Despite then receiving normal town status Crewe continued to be influenced by the railway presence for many years, the latter supplying its water until 1938 and its gas right up to 1952. The railway gift of a park and a hospital were also part of the relationship.

Swindon has a similar background of providing for the physical, spiritual and social well-being of a large railway community. When the works opened in 1843 the population of the old town, well south of the railway, was less than 2,500 but in fifty years the Swindon community grew to 32,839 of which over 80 per cent lived in the area around the works. The townspeople for many years distinguished between those who worked there and were 'inside' (ie the works, not prison), and others who were not. Among the many examples of social caring by the Great Western Railway Board was the provision of a small library which led, in its turn, to the building of the Mechanics Institute so that older students could continue their education.

To a smaller extent many other communities were affected by a railway presence. They derived a significant contribution to their rates and often depended on the railway for a sizeable part of the employment prospects. Cabbies or taxi drivers were needed to meet trains as well as men to work directly for the railways. Towns like Worcester, Caerphilly, Doncaster and Peterborough, together with districts like Stratford in East London and Springburn in Glasgow, had many compensations for accepting the noise and grime which came with the railway presence. Other towns benefited from housing industries serving the railway, Rugby, Newton-le-Willows and Chippenham being among the numerous examples.

The early railways were quite enlightened employers by the standards of the times, although there were exceptions and some companies were less organised than others. Some lines might not be sure just how old some of their staff were and the well-preserved could often continue at work as long as they could carry out their jobs. There was a tendency to treat staff as well as the profits would allow

Swindon

The Great Western Railway company town catered for the complete well being, both physical and spiritual, of all its employees

Swindon station where the private refreshment rooms were so little loved. The buildings are the original ones

The church built at Swindon for the spiritual well-being of the Great Western Railway employees there

The Mechanics Institute adjacent to substantial railway workers' housing

The main tunnel entrance to Swindon works in London Street

Midland and Royal Hotel at Gloucester

and the resultant differences in conditions caused quite a few problems in the grouping process. The Great Western, for example, found that the staff of the wealthy Barry Railway were accustomed to very different treatment from those of the poorer Midland and South Western Junction Railway.

The Great Western Railway, as one of the better railway employers, had started contributing to the Great Western Railway Provident Society soon after it was set up in 1838 and quite attractive pension funds were eventually to develop from this early beginning. Another early scheme was the Locomotive Department Sick Fund launched in the year that Swindon Works opened and also marking the beginning of an extensive provision for staff suffering from injury or ill health. The railway was also active in other areas of staff well-being, the savings bank which started with a membership of 900 and deposits of £16,000 growing to a membership of 23,000 with £2,500,000 on deposit by 1934.

From quite early on Great Western Railway station masters received an allowance to recognise the need for them to live near the job and the company later purchased houses for this purpose, £324 being spent on the one at Blagdon in 1908 and £432 for a house at Athelney in 1912. In the early 1920s it moved into the field of mortgages, offering up to 90 per cent of valuation at 5 per cent and for a period not exceeding twenty years. Staff could arrange to make repayments by means of a deduction through the paybills. Next came a plan for the letting of houses through a chain of public utility societies under which the railway advanced around £675,000 on 1,500 houses and some £80,000 was advanced by tenants as their investment in the societies, repayable on termination of a tenancy. The estate at Acton, still in use for accommodating railway staff, was under the control of the Great Western (London) Garden Village Society and the Great Western Railway described its standards in the following words:

> There are two main classes of houses differing slightly in accommodation and design. Nearly all are semi-detached and no block contains more than four. The average rents of the two types [in 1935] are 10s 5d and 12s 7d. Sub-letting is discouraged because it leads to overcrowding. No house contains two families and lodgers are allowed only on terms.

The railways also provided accommodation, albeit in a different form, through their very considerable hotel activity. In the Great Western's case the company's pride and joy was the Great Western Hotel at Paddington, another piece of enterprise deriving from the fertile brain of Brunel who saw the hotel as an integral part of the facility for conveying passengers from New York to London and back via the lines and associated liners of the Great Western Railway. The hotel was financed by a group of Great Western Railway directors and was completed in June 1852 to the designs of Philip Charles Hardwick RA, its Louis XIV towers rising seven storeys high and framing the main building with its 112 bedrooms, 15 sitting rooms and collection of public rooms, lounges and restaurant.

In 1933 the London, Midland and Scottish Railway could, and did, claim to have the largest hotel business in Europe. Building upon what it had absorbed from the Midland Railway, the company had come to own and manage no less than twenty-seven major hotels, among them some of the great names for luxurious and comfortable living. Gleneagles, Turnberry, the Adelphi at Liverpool and the Midland at Manchester could all, quite reasonably, be described as palatial and the atmosphere of hotels like the Caledonian at Edinburgh captured the essence of an era. Amid spacious rooms and foyers the guests could relax or conduct their business with every furnishing designed to comfort and every member of the staff there to anticipate or respond to their needs. The Caledonian was noted for its 'dinner dancing', responding early to this post-Armistice phenomenon and engaging an orchestra to help diners dance down the enormous meals available in the restaurant.

Some of the other companies catered more specifically for everyday needs. Lines like the Great Central and Great Eastern tended to have a prestige hotel in London and practical hotels elsewhere. In addition to its Great Eastern Hotel at Liverpool Street the Great Eastern Railway had built or purchased functional but comfortable hotels at Harwich to serve ferry passengers and Hunstanton to cater for the holiday trade, later adding the Felix Hotel at Felixstowe. The Great Central had a hotel of that name in London, the Royal Victoria Station Hotel at Sheffield, functional hotels at Grimsby, and the Victoria Station Hotel at Nottingham which had some fairly specific patrons in mind.

The close relationship between transport and accommodation which had existed in the stage coach era continued in the railway era. Many hotels advertised in the railway timetables and there were 'Station Hotel' signs all over the country. Many hotels and public houses took the name of their local railway company and others, further away from the station itself, provided gigs or omnibuses to connect with the most important trains. Some, like the Cross Keys Hotel at St Neots, were still providing this facility at the time of nationalisation. Others, like the New Passage Hotel on the Severn Estuary, had given up their railway connection, in this case when the Severn Tunnel ended the former rail and ferry service across to Portskewett. The New Passage Hotel itself remained in business until recent years and provided an interesting example of 'period' hotel accommodation, with impressive and spacious rooms overlooking the estuary for the first class passengers, smaller rooms above for those travelling second class, tiny boxes for the third class travellers and even smaller rooms, high up at the back, for the hotel serving staff.

The same combination of direct ownership and co-operation existed in the shipping sphere. The London and Blackwall Railway on the Thames and the Glasgow, Paisley and Greenock Railway on the Clyde had been involved with steamer services right from the beginning and the railways running to the South Coast were soon projecting the rail traffic activity into the deeper waters of the English Channel. Even before it had completed the final portion of its route from Ashford to Dover the South Eastern Railway had made an arrangement with the New Commercial Steam Packet Company so that passengers for the Continent could use a combined rail-coach-steamer service. Although the railways at first had no powers to operate steamer services themselves it was not long before they obtained these and by 1853 the South Eastern Railway had taken direct control of the three routes and eight vessels it had been operating through a subsidiary. The London and South Western company had done much the same thing, sponsoring the South Western Steam Packet Company to provide a service from Southampton to the Channel Islands and France.

Even modest concerns like the Somerset and Dorset Railway got involved in the shipping business and in the peak years dozens of services operated to the Continent, to Ireland, to the Isle of Man and the other offshore islands, across estuaries and on lakes and lochs. Some rationalisation took place at grouping —

Humber ferry vessel PS Tattershall Castle *leaving Hull for New Holland*

With a background of naval vessels 'Great Western Railway Steam Ferry' The Mew *is at work between Kingswear and Dartmouth*

one example being the merging of the joint Lancashire and Yorkshire and London and North Western service between Fleetwood and Belfast with the Heysham-Belfast service — but the big four still had very substantial shipping activities. In the case of the London, Midland and Scottish Railway the new company's marine superintendent was responsible for five deep sea routes, a pattern of services on the Clyde and such inland vessels as the elegant steamers at work on Lake Windermere. The railway vessels were an incredible mixture ranging from Thames ferries to cross channel packets and from Clyde paddlers to train ferry vessels. But travelling on them was an event to be savoured and anyone who has waited for a paddle steamer to tie up at Wemyss Bay or Ardrossan in a strong cross wind or seen a stoker on one of the Humber ferries lift shovel after shovel of coal to the shoulder-level furnaces will not forget the experience.

The railways had a close liaison with many private shipping companies in addition to their own direct interests. By arrangements with the Isle of Man Steam Packet Company through bookings could be made to Douglas, while the Isles of Scilly Steamship Company was the railway agent on the islands for both passenger travel and for arranging the combined steamer and rail movement of the thousands of bunches of early daffodils grown on the temperate Scillies. All sorts of rail and steamer excursions were operated, especially with larger owners like General Steam Navigation whose vessels would give the London day tripper the relaxation of a leisurely trip down river to Southend before spending the day in the sun and the evening among the Kursall entertainments. He could then take the late train home and sleep off some of the day's excesses on the journey back to Liverpool Street or Fenchurch Street.

The extensive and complex railway dock activities further extended the

Export coal being loaded to ship at Grangemouth

An impression of the railway view of the docks activity can be obtained from the extensive railway literature on the subject and the following is just a small extract from the substantial 1938 edition of *Ports of the LNER*:

THE LONDON & NORTH EASTERN RAILWAY COMPANY'S HULL DOCK SYSTEM

It was towards the end of the eighteenth century that the Hull Dock Company began building docks in Hull, the oldest being those almost in the centre of the city known as the Queen's (now filled in), Humber, and Prince's Docks. Then followed the Railway, Victoria, Albert and William Wright, and St Andrew's Docks. Railway communication with Hull was first effected in 1840, when the Hull and Selby Railway (now part of the London and North Eastern system) was opened. The Hull and Barnsley Railway, now also amalgamated with the London and North Eastern, started working in July 1885, almost simultaneously with the opening of the Alexandra Dock, which, under the powers contained in the Act of Parliament incorporating the railway, was constructed by the Hull and Barnsley Company. This dock was the largest on the Humber until the opening, in the summer of 1914, of the King George Dock, the joint property of the then Hull and Barnsley and North Eastern Companies. The North Eastern Railway (also now a part of the London and North Eastern system) first became dock-owners in Hull in 1893, when the old Hull Dock Company disposed of their property to the railway company. The latter have since carried out many improvements in the dock and riverside facilities, and were instrumental in finding capital for the King George Dock. The London and North Eastern Company are now, of course, sole owners of the Hull Docks, covering a total water area of 210 acres, with approximately 600 acres of open storage space, 12 miles of quays, and a river frontage of over seven miles. The docks are equipped with handling appliances of the most up-to-date character, and possess large warehouses for the storage of grain, seed, wool, and general goods, their total capacity being upwards of 350,000 quarters of grain and 207,000 tons of general goods. All the quays have rail connexion, and most of them are furnished with transit sheds.

companies' marine interests. Their own docks represented significant sources of revenue from the various dues payable and both these and the other major ports contributed vast volumes of traffic to and from the railway system. Some of the figures involved are hardly comprehendable: figures like 38 million tons of coal exported through the South Wales ports in 1913; 900 million bananas imported through Avonmouth in 1930; 9,000 vessels using the Tyne in 1935 and producing trade worth £23,068,757; 7,000 barges available daily in the PLA docks . . . . With a host of supplementary activities deriving from grain silos, timber ponds, bonded stores and other such facilities, and most of the non-local business moving by rail, ports and shipping represented an important facet of the railway scene right up to nationalisation.

The year 1933 not only saw the introduction of the Great Western Railway's air service but also the experimental introduction of the first streamlined AEC

The Great Western Railway was also a pioneer of air transport

SEEKING to anticipate the needs of the travelling public, and not regarding themselves merely as carriers by rail, but as providers of transport, the Great Western Railway Company promoted a Bill in Parliament to acquire powers for the transport of passengers and goods by air. The Bill passed through its various stages and received the Royal Assent on 10 May 1929, another type of transport thus being added to the older forms.

The first actual use of the powers obtained was not made until 1933. On 3 April of that year *The Times* announced that, commencing on 12 April, a regular daily air service would be operated for the Great Western Railway Company between Cardiff, Teignmouth, Torquay, and Plymouth. This was the first air service in the British Isles operated on behalf of any of the railway companies, and wide possibilities were opened up for the transport of passengers, freight, and mail by co-operation between the older forms of transport by rail, road, and sea, with the newest practicable method of transport by air.

It will readily be appreciated that between many important towns in the British Isles the only way of obtaining rapid transit is by air, owing to the geographical position of the towns, and a good instance of this was demonstrated by the route selected for the original service. Passengers travelling by rail or road from Cardiff must make a detour *via* Bristol when travelling to Devon or Cornwall, owing to the Bristol Channel, but by air passengers between these points make a direct journey, taking less than half the time occupied in a rail journey.

Though the number of aerodromes is very limited, the Great Western Railway began at once to do everything possible to co-ordinate the two forms of transport. For instance, aircraft were so scheduled to arrive at Plymouth airport that passengers could be conveyed by road to the railway station and continue a journey to Cornwall by rail, saving many hours on the journey. Permission was subsequently given by the Postmaster-General for the carriage of mails by air, and this was actually begun on 15 May, the first authorized regular air mail service in the British Isles. The air service was regarded as experimental, and it was decided to extend the route to Birmingham, and with the beginning of that service on 22 May 1933, the distance between the terminal points was exactly doubled.

The air service was suspended on 29 September 1933, and in the following months the experience gained was closely examined, with the result that in March 1934, a new company was formed called Railway Air Services Limited, in which the four main line railway companies and Imperial Airways Limited, were participants. Operations in 1934 were begun on 7 May, with a route from Plymouth to Liverpool, calling at Teignmouth, Cardiff, and Birmingham, this being an extension of the route operated in 1933. In July of the same year further developments took place with the opening of a route from Birmingham to Cowes, Isle of Wight, calling at Bristol and Southampton, this route being jointly run with the Southern Railway Company.

148

Shunting horse at work

diesel railcar which went to work on local services between Paddington, Reading and Didcot. It was part of the high Great Western Railway awareness of the need to cater for local traffic which had started back in 1903 with the Helston — Lizard bus service and the parallel development of the 'halts' policy, inaugurated on 12 October of that year with the first steam rail motor service, between Chalford and Stonehouse. Some of the later Great Western Railway bus services led to the closure of its own branches — the Welshpool and Llanfair line is an example — and generally neither railcars nor buses, nor even the experiments with a mutation of both, did more than slow down the tide of increasing road encroachment into the local travel business.

The railways' road activities in connection with goods traffic fared rather better and both service and advertising messages were displayed all over the country. The original cartage activities involved using horses and drays and the London and North Eastern Railway, which had had 1,743 horses clip-clopping the streets of the larger cities in 1939, still employed 1,280 in 1947. But by then the cost of a horse had risen from £57 to £87 and its daily consumption of oats and bran, hay and clover mixture, 1lb of beans and 30lbs of mixed provender was proving a costly factor. The problem of keeping extra horses at strategic points to help with heavy loads where the return to the depot involved a hill, the stabling requirements and the decreasing numbers of men wanting to work with horses were other pertinent factors, although horses continued to work at depots like Deansgate, Manchester and over 100 were still performing shunting duties at the time of the 1947 Transport Act.

While the trains, ships and planes served the needs of travellers and industry it

Typical railway scene in the steam age – hard working locomotive, heavy train, goods yard behind, dozens of signals and quite a few signal boxes

G.W.R. SERIES OF TRAVEL BOOKS

"The Literature of Locomotion"—*Vide* "THE OBSERVER."

THE travel books published by the G.W.R. have become widely known as "The Holiday Books of the Holiday Line." They are unique in railway literature, and form an exceedingly popular series of literary hand-books owing to the thoroughly practical, and at the same time interesting, manner in which the information is presented. All the travel books are printed in best style, beautifully illustrated, and each contains a beautiful map.

List of Classical Travel Books

THE CORNISH RIVIERA : OUR NATIONAL HEALTH AND PLEASURE RESORT. A travel book dealing fully with Cornwall, the land of beauty and romance. Price 6d., by post 9d.

DEVON : THE SHIRE OF THE SEA KINGS. New edition in course of preparation. Price 6d., by post 9d.

HISTORIC SITES AND SCENES OF ENGLAND. This publication tells the story of England's glorious history, so far as it touches the unrivalled sites and scenes served by the G.W.R. Price 6d., by post 11d.

NORTH WALES : THE BRITISH TYROL. Letterpress and pictures go to prove that in North Wales England possesses a Tyrol of its own. Price 6d., by post 9d.

SOUTH WALES : THE COUNTRY OF CASTLES. Relates in an interesting style the delights of travel in this romantic part of the Principality. Price 6d., by post 9d.

CATHEDRALS. Describes the Cathedrals on the Great Western Railway ; 74 full-page illustrations, 51 black-and-white drawings. Price 2s. 6d., post free 3s.

RURAL LONDON. Contains much data relating to the delightful country between Paddington and Reading. Price 6d., post free 9d.

106

List of G.W.R. Hand-books and Booklets

THE CAMBRIAN COAST. THE WEST COAST OF WALES FROM PWLLHELI TO TENBY. Beautifully illustrated and complete with Railway Map. Price 6d., by post 8d.

THROUGH THE WINDOW. A delightful book describing over 300 miles of scenery and places of interest as seen through the railway carriage window on a journey from Paddington to Penzance. 54 maps, 164 illustrations and 8 beautiful plates. Price 1s., by post 1s. 3d.

LEGENDLAND. (4 Volumes) Each Volume contains twelve unique and inspiring tales, an ancient West Country folk-song, illustrations and maps. Price 6d. each Volume, by post 8d. each, or the four for 2s. 6d.

These books may be obtained at the Company's principal stations and Offices at the prices shown, or will be forwarded on application to the office of the Superintendent of the Line, G.W.R., PADDINGTON STATION, LONDON, W.2, on receipt of stamps.

The G.W.R. have published a series of small illustrated booklets, giving a variety of useful information in a condensed form. These dainty little volumes, which may be obtained free of charge (postage 2d.), have received the highest commendations from the Press on both sides of the Atlantic, are entitled—

1. The Cornish Riviera.
2. Devon—The Lovely Land of the "Mayflower."
3. Shakespeare Land.
4. Wonderful Wessex.
5. Places of Pilgrimage.
6. The Wye Valley (Hereford to Chepstow).
7. The Severn Valley.
8. Cornwall and its Wild Life.
9. The Wye Valley (Plinlimmon to Hereford).

OTHER FREE BOOKLETS—

Camping Holidays on the G.W.R.
Inland and Marine Spas.
Winter Resorts on the G.W.R.

Sunny Cornwall.
The Glories of the Thames.
Wessex White Horses.
Welsh Mountain Railways.

These Books will be forwarded on application to the Office of the Superintendent of the Line, G.W.R., PADDINGTON STATION, LONDON, W.2, on receipt of stamps.

107

A summary of some of the Great Western Railway publicity

was the cartage fleet and the publicity department that kept them in the public eye. One would not spend long in the average town without seeing either a horse and dray or its successor the mechanical horse. In country areas there would be pugnacious Albions with a load of grain, sleek Bedfords picking up the milk churns, double decker livestock lorries bearing the legend 'Livestock Carted to and from Farm, Market and Station', Great Western Railway vehicles increasing their load capacity by towing a two-wheel trailer and London and North Eastern Railway 2-ton Morris Commercials working a parcels round so regularly you could nearly set your watch by them. The Great Western Railway used a road motor for a publicity tour of Scotland as early as 1908 and in later years cartage vehicles were provided with poster boards so that they could display the railway message on their to-ings and fro-ings.

The publicity activity produced a great many posters for use on stations and off station sites and many are now appreciated as fine examples of an interesting art form. A great deal of literature was also produced and no company went further than the Great Western Railway in spreading its message through leaflets, booklets, book marks, jigsaws and the like.

For every obtrusive railway activity there was an unobtrusive one. Only the army knew how much work the railways did through the connections with the military railways and few people would suspect that a census on the London, Midland and Scottish Railway in 1927 revealed that over 11,000 men and women had passed examinations held under the auspices of the company's ambulance movement. Through the agency of the great railways you could travel from Penzance to Thurso or take a ship to Europe; you could send your goods the length and breadth of the nation, be they small parcels or giant stators; you could get arrested by the railway police for trespassing or entrust the movement of something as complex as a zoo or art collection to the local company.

Many of these things one can still do, of course, but freight and passenger movement is now a thing of speed and efficiency and if sometimes in the past it was neither, it was always colourful especially when viewed with hindsight.

INDEX

TRANSPORT BOOKS FROM MOORLAND PUBLISHING

Portraits of 'Castles'
B. Holden & K. Leech
A study of the Great Western Railway *Castle* class locomotives. This is the first comprehensive illustrated book dealing with them all.

Portraits of 'Kings'
B. Holden & K. Leech
The first complete photographic record of every *King* class locomotive.

An Illustrated History of Preserved Railways
G. Body
The story of Britain's railways and the preservation schemes that keep alive the spirit of the steam age.

Building Britain's Locomotives
J.W. Lowe
A photographic study of all the stages involved in the construction of Britain's locomotives from Victorian times to the end of steam.

The Branch Line Age
C.J. Gammel
Nostalgic photographs recall the days of Britain's branch lines before the 'Beeching Axe'.

British Locomotive Catalogue 1825-1923
D. Baxter
Volumes of the invaluable reference series now available include:
1   Summary and index
2A and 2B London and North Western Railway
3A   Midland
3B   Lancashire & Yorkshire

Narrow Boats at Work
M.E. Ware
Life and work on Britain's canals portrayed in historic photographs.

Britain's Canal & River Craft
E. Paget-Tomlinson
Almost every type of craft that have worked on the inland waterways is described and illustrated.

Guide to Stationary Steam Engines
G. Hayes
A description of all those engines which may be visited.

These are just a few titles from our current booklist (send SAE) which includes books on transport, sport, architecture, collecting, guidebooks, countryside, etc.

Available from good bookshops or write to:
MOORLAND PUBLISHING CO LTD,
PO Box 2, 9-11 Station Street,
Ashbourne, Derbyshire, DE6 1DZ.